D1079496

ATLAS
OF THE
WORLD

KINGFISHER
Kingfisher Publications Plc
New Penderel House, 283–288 High Holborn,
London WC1V 7HZ

First published in hardback by Kingfisher Publications Plc 1997
10 9 8 7 6 5 4 3 2 1

Firts published in paperback 1998
10 9 8 7 6 5 4 3 2
2TR(1BFC)/0699/MID/NEW(NEW)/128JAMA

Copyright © Kingfisher Publications Plc 1997

A CIP catalogue record for this book is available from the
British Library.

ISBN 0 7534 0137 1 (hb)
ISBN 0 7534 0275 0 (pb)
Printed in Hong Kong

Produced by Miles Kelly Publishing Ltd
Designer: Smiljka Surla
Editors: Rosie Alexander, Samantha Armstrong,
    Angela Royston
Assistant Editor: Susanne Bull
Picture Research: Kate Miles, Yannick Yago

ATLAS
OF THE
WORLD

Philip Steele

KINGfISHER

Contents

How to use a map

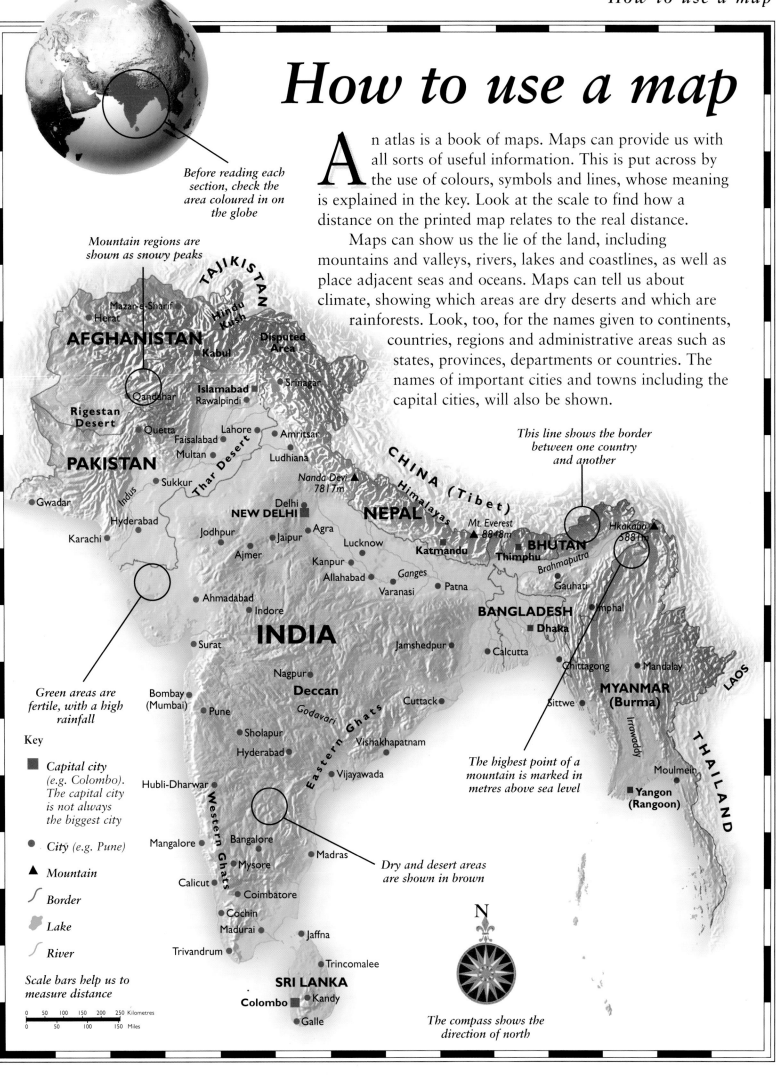

An atlas is a book of maps. Maps can provide us with all sorts of useful information. This is put across by the use of colours, symbols and lines, whose meaning is explained in the key. Look at the scale to find how a distance on the printed map relates to the real distance.

Maps can show us the lie of the land, including mountains and valleys, rivers, lakes and coastlines, as well as place adjacent seas and oceans. Maps can tell us about climate, showing which areas are dry deserts and which are rainforests. Look, too, for the names given to continents, countries, regions and administrative areas such as states, provinces, departments or countries. The names of important cities and towns including the capital cities, will also be shown.

Before reading each section, check the area coloured in on the globe

Mountain regions are shown as snowy peaks

This line shows the border between one country and another

Green areas are fertile, with a high rainfall

The highest point of a mountain is marked in metres above sea level

Dry and desert areas are shown in brown

Key

■ *Capital city (e.g. Colombo). The capital city is not always the biggest city*

● *City (e.g. Pune)*

▲ *Mountain*

∫ *Border*

Lake

∫ *River*

Scale bars help us to measure distance

0 50 100 150 200 250 Kilometres

0 50 100 150 Miles

The compass shows the direction of north

TAJIKISTAN

Mazar-e-Sharif
Herat
AFGHANISTAN
Hindu Kush
Kabul
Disputed Area
Srinagar
Qandahar
Islamabad
Rawalpindi
Rigestan Desert
Quetta
Lahore
Amritsar
Faisalabad
Multan
Ludhiana
PAKISTAN
Thar Desert
Sukkur
Nanda Devi ▲ 7817m
CHINA (Tibet)
Gwadar
Indus
Delhi
NEPAL
Himalayas
Mt. Everest ▲ 8848m
Hkakabo ▲ 5881m
Hyderabad
NEW DELHI ■
Agra
Jodhpur
Jaipur
Lucknow
Katmandu
BHUTAN
Karachi
Ajmer
Kanpur
Thimphu
Brahmaputra
Allahabad
Ganges
Patna
Gauhati
Ahmadabad
Varanasi
BANGLADESH
Imphal
Indore
Dhaka ■
Surat
INDIA
Jamshedpur
Calcutta
Nagpur
Chittagong
Mandalay
LAOS
Bombay (Mumbai)
Deccan
Cuttack
MYANMAR (Burma)
Pune
Godavari
Sittwe
Sholapur
Eastern Ghats
Vishakhapatnam
Irrawaddy
Hyderabad
Vijayawada
THAILAND
Hubli-Dharwar
Western Ghats
Mangalore
Bangalore
Moulmein
Mysore
Madras
Calicut
Yangon (Rangoon) ■
Coimbatore
Cochin
Madurai
Jaffna
Trivandrum
Trincomalee
SRI LANKA
Colombo ■ Kandy
Galle

N

Maps and mapmaking

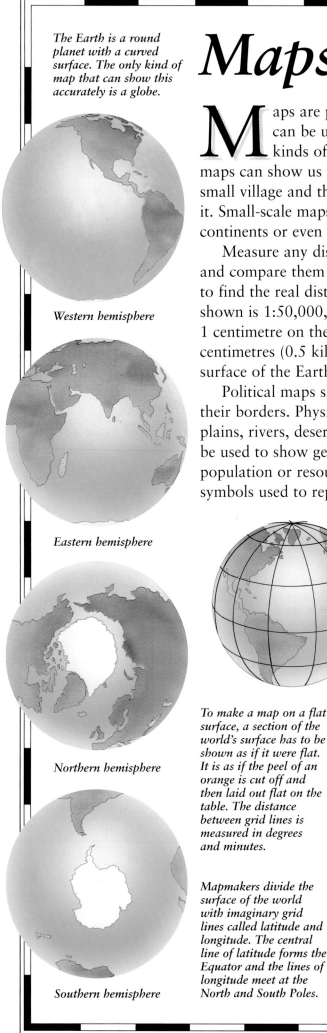

The Earth is a round planet with a curved surface. The only kind of map that can show this accurately is a globe.

Western hemisphere

Eastern hemisphere

Northern hemisphere

Southern hemisphere

Maps are plans of the land around us. They can be used to show many different kinds of information. Large-scale maps can show us the streets of a town or a small village and the countryside around it. Small-scale maps can fit in countries, continents or even the whole world.

Measure any distances on the maps and compare them with the bar scale to find the real distance. If the scale shown is 1:50,000, it means that 1 centimetre on the map equals 50,000 centimetres (0.5 kilometres) on the surface of the Earth.

Political maps show countries or states and their borders. Physical maps show mountains, plains, rivers, deserts and forests. Maps can also be used to show geology, vegetation, climate, population or resources. A key normally shows the symbols used to represent features on the map.

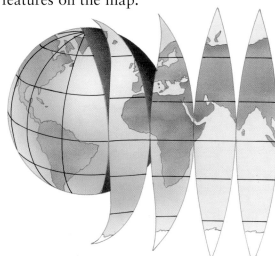

A globe

To make a map on a flat surface, a section of the world's surface has to be shown as if it were flat. It is as if the peel of an orange is cut off and then laid out flat on the table. The distance between grid lines is measured in degrees and minutes.

Mapmakers transfer the curving grids of the Earth's surface to a grid plan drawn on a flat sheet or screen. There are various ways they can do this. Each method is called a projection. No projection can be completely accurate. Maps normally show north at the top and south at the bottom – but they do not have to!

Mapmakers divide the surface of the world with imaginary grid lines called latitude and longitude. The central line of latitude forms the Equator and the lines of longitude meet at the North and South Poles.

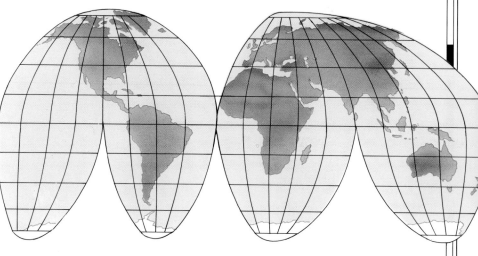

The Earth

The Earth is a great ball of rock that spins around as it travels through space. It is one of the nine planets that, together with asteroids and comets, travel around our local star, which we call the Sun. The Sun, a fiercely hot ball of gas, provides the Earth with warmth and light. The atmosphere, a layer of gases that surrounds the Earth, shields us from some of the Sun's more harmful rays. It also provides the air which makes it possible for people to live on Earth.

PLANET EARTH
Circumference around the Equator: 40,075 kilometres
Circumference around the Poles: 40,008 kilometres
Diameter at the Equator: 12,756 kilometres
Surface area: About 510,000,000 square kilometres
Area covered by sea: 71 percent
Average distance from the Sun: 149,600,000 kilometres
Average distance from the Moon: 385,000 kilometres
Period of rotation: 23 hours 56 minutes
Speed of rotation: 1,660 kilometres per hour at the Equator
Period of revolution: 365 days 6 hours
Speed of revolution: 29.8 kilometres per second

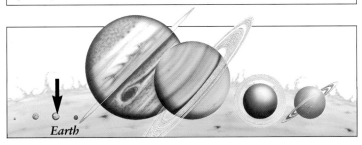

Earth

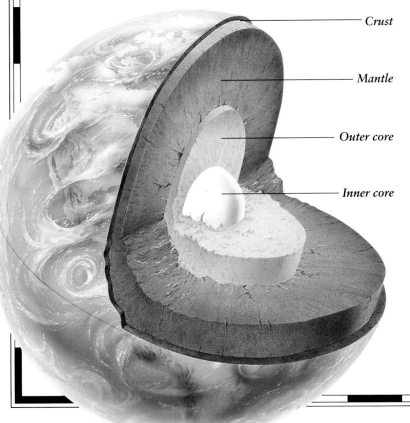

Crust

Mantle

Outer core

Inner core

HIGHEST PEAKS

Mountain	Height	Location
Everest (Qomolangma)	*8,848 m*	*China-Nepal*
K2 (Qogir Feng)	*8,611 m*	*India-Pakistan*
Kanchenjunga	*8,586 m*	*India-Nepal*
Makalu 1	*8,463 m*	*China-Nepal*
Dhaulagiri 1	*8,167 m*	*Nepal*
Nanga Parbat	*8,125 m*	*India*
Annapurna 1	*8,091 m*	*Nepal*
Gosainthan (Xixabangma Feng)	*8,012 m*	*China*
Distaghil Sar	*7,885 m*	*India*
Nanda Devi	*7,816 m*	*India*

LONGEST RIVERS

River	Length	Location
Nile	*6,670 km*	*North Africa*
Amazon	*6,448 km*	*South America*
Chang Jiang (Yangtze)	*6,300 km*	*Central China*
Mississippi-Missouri-Red	*6,020 km*	*North America*
Yenisey-Angara-Selenga	*5,540 km*	*Mongolia-Russia*
Huang He	*5,464 km*	*Northern China*
Ob-Irtysh	*5,409 km*	*Russia-Kazakhstan*
Congo	*4,700 km*	*Central Africa*
Lena-Kirenga	*4,400 km*	*Russia*
Mekong	*4,350 km*	*Southeast Asia*

LARGEST LAKES

Lake	Area	Location
Caspian Sea	*371,800 sq km*	*Central Asia*
Superior	*82,103 sq km*	*USA-Canada*
Victoria	*69,484 sq km*	*East Africa*
Aral Sea	*65,500 sq km*	*Central Asia*
Huron	*59,569 sq km*	*USA-Canada*
Michigan	*57,757 sq km*	*USA-Canada*
Tanganyika	*32,893 sq km*	*East Africa*
Baikal	*31,449 sq km*	*Russia*
Great Bear	*31,328 sq km*	*Canada*
Malawi	*28,878 sq km*	*Southern Africa*

LARGEST ISLANDS

Island	Area
Greenland	*2,175,600 sq km*
New Guinea	*821,000 sq km*
Borneo	*727,900 sq km*
Madagascar	*589,081 sq km*
Baffin	*509,214 sq km*
Sumatra	*431,982 sq km*
Honshu	*228,204 sq km*
Great Britain	*218,800 sq km*
Victoria	*212,200 sq km*
Ellesmere	*196,917 sq km*

MAJOR WATERFALLS

Highest Waterfalls	Height	Location
Angel Falls	*979 m*	*Venezuela*
Mardsalsfossen	*774 m*	*Norway*
Yosemite	*739 m*	*United States*

Greatest volume Waterfall	Volume	Location
Boyoma	*17,000 cu m per sec*	*Democratic Republic of Congo*

OCEANS

Name	Area
Pacific	*180,000,000 sq km*
Atlantic	*106,000,000 sq km*
Indian	*73,500,000 sq km*
Arctic	*14,350,000 sq km*

Countries of the World

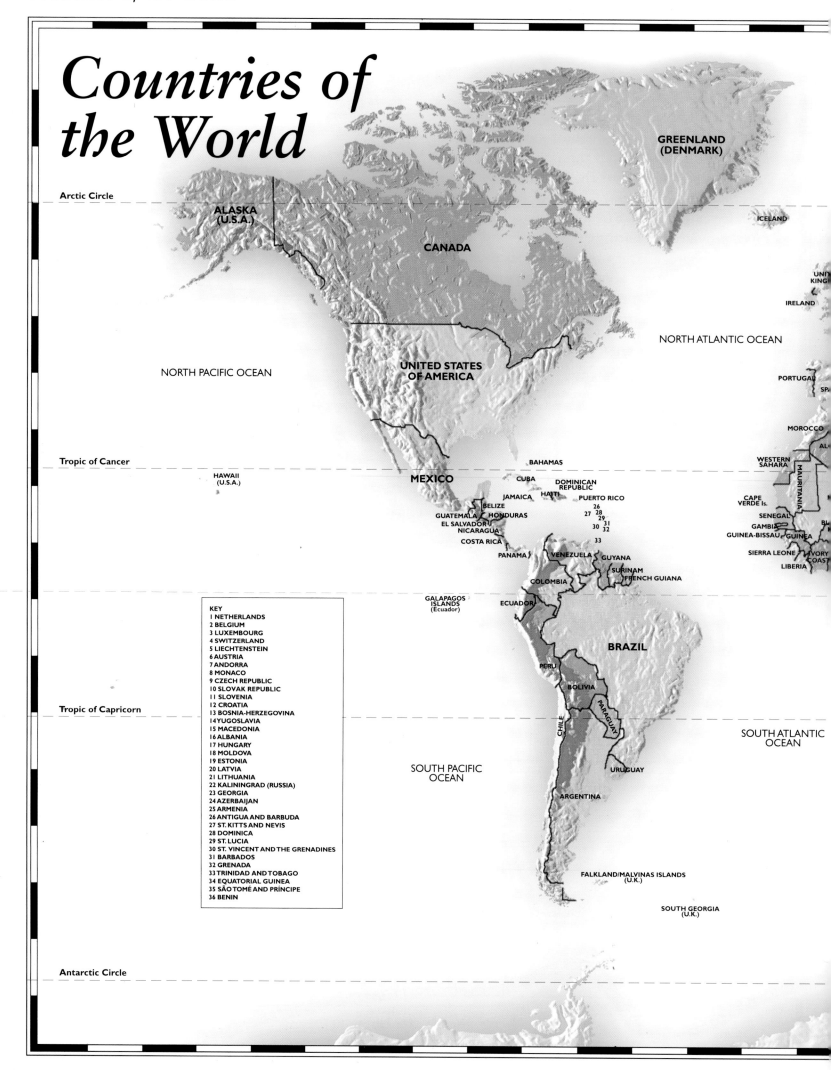

Arctic Circle

GREENLAND
(DENMARK)

ICELAND

ALASKA
(U.S.A.)

CANADA

UNITED
KING

IRELAND

NORTH ATLANTIC OCEAN

NORTH PACIFIC OCEAN

UNITED STATES
OF AMERICA

PORTUGAL

SPA

Tropic of Cancer

MOROCCO

BAHAMAS

WESTERN
SAHARA

HAWAII
(U.S.A.)

MEXICO

CUBA

DOMINICAN
REPUBLIC

JAMAICA   HAITI

PUERTO RICO

26

27   28
      29
30   31
       32

CAPE
VERDE Is.

SENEGAL

MAURITANIA

BELIZE

GUATEMALA   HONDURAS
EL SALVADOR
NICARAGUA

COSTA RICA

33

PANAMA

GAMBIA
GUINEA-BISSAU   GUINEA

SIERRA LEONE   IVORY
                COAST

LIBERIA

VENEZUELA   GUYANA
          SURINAM
          FRENCH GUIANA

GALAPAGOS
ISLANDS
(Ecuador)

COLOMBIA

ECUADOR

KEY
1 NETHERLANDS
2 BELGIUM
3 LUXEMBOURG
4 SWITZERLAND
5 LIECHTENSTEIN
6 AUSTRIA
7 ANDORRA
8 MONACO
9 CZECH REPUBLIC
10 SLOVAK REPUBLIC
11 SLOVENIA
12 CROATIA
13 BOSNIA-HERZEGOVINA
14 YUGOSLAVIA
15 MACEDONIA
16 ALBANIA
17 HUNGARY
18 MOLDOVA
19 ESTONIA
20 LATVIA
21 LITHUANIA
22 KALININGRAD (RUSSIA)
23 GEORGIA
24 AZERBAIJAN
25 ARMENIA
26 ANTIGUA AND BARBUDA
27 ST. KITTS AND NEVIS
28 DOMINICA
29 ST. LUCIA
30 ST. VINCENT AND THE GRENADINES
31 BARBADOS
32 GRENADA
33 TRINLAND AND TOBAGO
34 EQUATORIAL GUINEA
35 SÃO TOMÉ AND PRÍNCIPE
36 BENIN

BRAZIL

PERU

BOLIVIA

PARAGUAY

Tropic of Capricorn

CHILE

SOUTH ATLANTIC
OCEAN

URUGUAY

SOUTH PACIFIC
OCEAN

ARGENTINA

FALKLAND/MALVINAS ISLANDS
(U.K.)

SOUTH GEORGIA
(U.K.)

Antarctic Circle

10

ARCTIC OCEAN

RUSSIA

NORTH PACIFIC OCEAN

SWEDEN
FINLAND
19
20
21
22
DENMARK
POLAND
BELARUS
GERMANY
9
10
UKRAINE
KAZAKHSTAN
MONGOLIA
17
ROMANIA
16
BULGARIA
23
24
UZBEKISTAN
KYRGYZSTAN
NORTH KOREA
ITALY
14
GREECE
TURKEY
TURKMENISTAN
TAJIKISTAN
SOUTH KOREA
JAPAN
TUNISIA
CYPRUS
SYRIA
AFGHANISTAN
CHINA
LEBANON
IRAQ
IRAN
ISRAEL
JORDAN
KUWAIT
PAKISTAN
LIBYA
EGYPT
BAHRAIN
QATAR
NEPAL
BHUTAN
TAIWAN
SAUDI ARABIA
UNITED ARAB EMIRATES
BANGLADESH
INDIA
OMAN
MYANMAR (BURMA)
LAOS
CHAD
SUDAN
ERITREA
YEMEN
THAILAND
VIETNAM
PHILIPPINES
CAMBODIA
CENTRAL AFRICAN REPUBLIC
CAMEROON
ETHIOPIA
SRI LANKA
MALDIVES
FED. STATES OF MICRONESIA
MARSHALL ISLANDS
PALAU
KIRIBATI
GABON
CONGO
UGANDA
SOMALIA
INDIAN OCEAN
BRUNEI
MALAYSIA
KENYA
SINGAPORE
TUVALU
RWANDA
DEMOCRATIC REPUBLIC OF CONGO
BURUNDI
TANZANIA
SEYCHELLES
PAPUA NEW GUINEA
INDONESIA
SOLOMON ISLANDS
SAMOA
ANGOLA
COMOROS
MALAWI
TONGA
ZAMBIA
MOZAMBIQUE
VANUATU
FIJI
NAMIBIA
ZIMBABWE
MADAGASCAR
MAURITIUS
BOTSWANA
RÉUNION (FR.)
NEW CALEDONIA (FR.)
SWAZILAND
AUSTRALIA
SOUTH AFRICA
LESOTHO

NEW ZEALAND

ANTARCTICA

0   1000   2000   3000   4000   5000   6000 Kilometres
0   1000   2000   3000   4000 Miles

The Continents

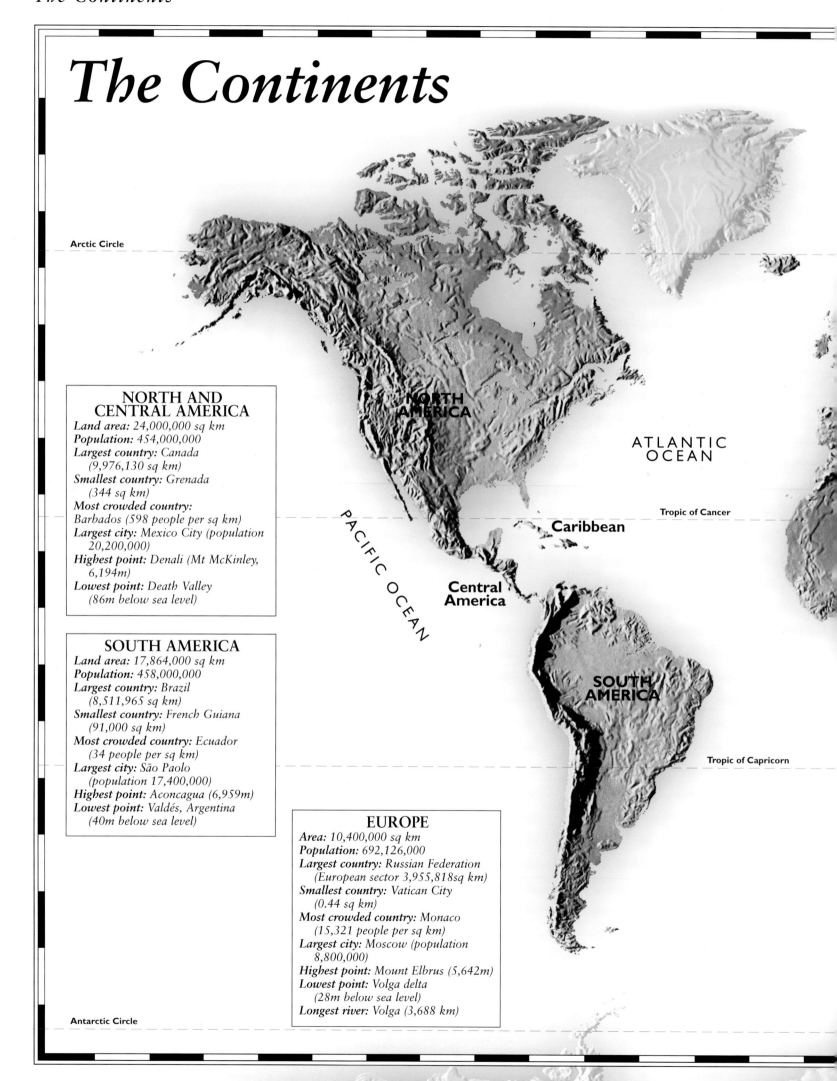

NORTH AND CENTRAL AMERICA

Land area: 24,000,000 sq km
Population: 454,000,000
Largest country: Canada
(9,976,130 sq km)
Smallest country: Grenada
(344 sq km)
Most crowded country:
Barbados (598 people per sq km)
Largest city: Mexico City (population
20,200,000)
Highest point: Denali (Mt McKinley,
6,194m)
Lowest point: Death Valley
(86m below sea level)

SOUTH AMERICA

Land area: 17,864,000 sq km
Population: 458,000,000
Largest country: Brazil
(8,511,965 sq km)
Smallest country: French Guiana
(91,000 sq km)
Most crowded country: Ecuador
(34 people per sq km)
Largest city: São Paolo
(population 17,400,000)
Highest point: Aconcagua (6,959m)
Lowest point: Valdés, Argentina
(40m below sea level)

EUROPE

Area: 10,400,000 sq km
Population: 692,126,000
Largest country: Russian Federation
(European sector 3,955,818sq km)
Smallest country: Vatican City
(0.44 sq km)
Most crowded country: Monaco
(15,321 people per sq km)
Largest city: Moscow (population
8,800,000)
Highest point: Mount Elbrus (5,642m)
Lowest point: Volga delta
(28m below sea level)
Longest river: Volga (3,688 km)

Arctic Circle

Tropic of Cancer

Tropic of Capricorn

Antarctic Circle

ATLANTIC
OCEAN

PACIFIC OCEAN

NORTH
AMERICA

Caribbean

Central
America

SOUTH
AMERICA

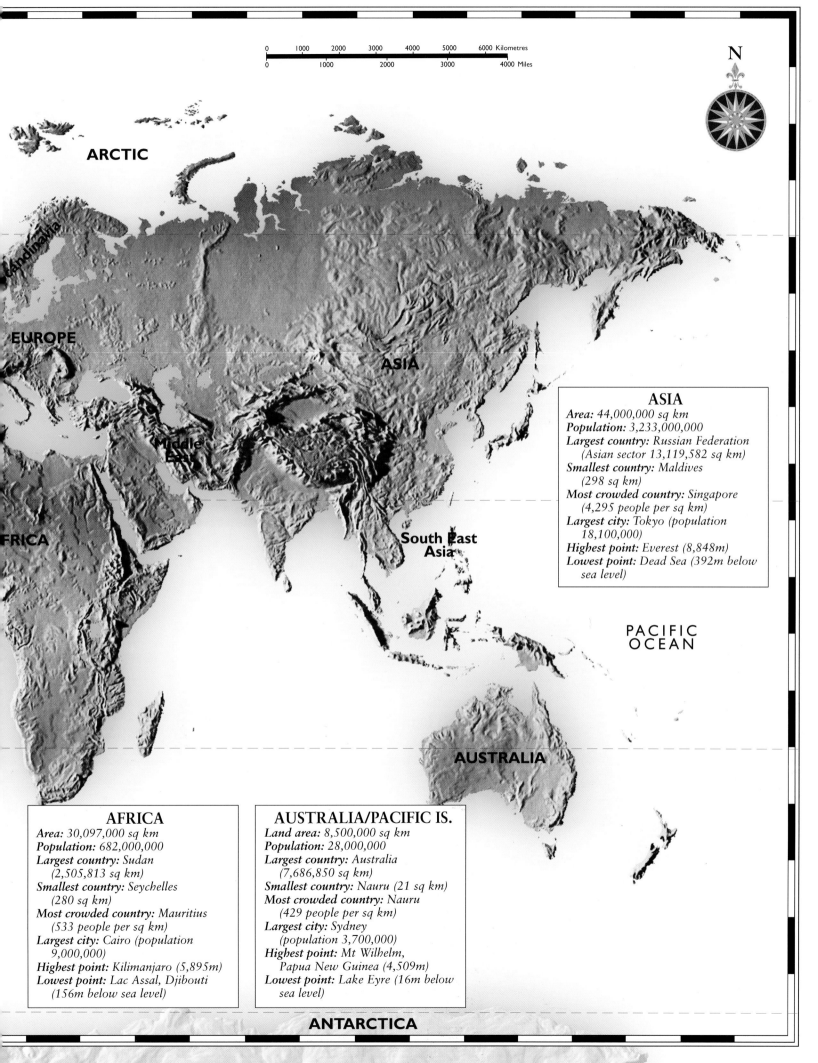

ARCTIC

Scandinavia

EUROPE

ASIA

Middle East

AFRICA

South East Asia

AUSTRALIA

PACIFIC OCEAN

ANTARCTICA

N

ASIA
Area: 44,000,000 sq km
Population: 3,233,000,000
Largest country: Russian Federation
   (Asian sector 13,119,582 sq km)
Smallest country: Maldives
   (298 sq km)
Most crowded country: Singapore
   (4,295 people per sq km)
Largest city: Tokyo (population
   18,100,000)
Highest point: Everest (8,848m)
Lowest point: Dead Sea (392m below
   sea level)

AFRICA
Area: 30,097,000 sq km
Population: 682,000,000
Largest country: Sudan
   (2,505,813 sq km)
Smallest country: Seychelles
   (280 sq km)
Most crowded country: Mauritius
   (533 people per sq km)
Largest city: Cairo (population
   9,000,000)
Highest point: Kilimanjaro (5,895m)
Lowest point: Lac Assal, Djibouti
   (156m below sea level)

AUSTRALIA/PACIFIC IS.
Land area: 8,500,000 sq km
Population: 28,000,000
Largest country: Australia
   (7,686,850 sq km)
Smallest country: Nauru (21 sq km)
Most crowded country: Nauru
   (429 people per sq km)
Largest city: Sydney
   (population 3,700,000)
Highest point: Mt Wilhelm,
   Papua New Guinea (4,509m)
Lowest point: Lake Eyre (16m below
   sea level)

Canada

Canada is a vast country, second only to the Russian Federation in area. And yet it is inhabited by only 28 million people, and they mostly live in the far south, along the United States border. The reason is that the far north of Canada is an icy wilderness, lying within the Arctic Circle. Nearly half of the country is covered by evergreen forest. Winters are severe throughout the country, but the brief summers may be warm, even in the Arctic.

The northern wilderness is rich in minerals, oil and gas, while the fertile prairies of the south form one of the world's most important wheat-growing regions. Cattle, timber, and fisheries are all important to the Canadian economy. Large cities such as Vancouver, Toronto and Montreal are major industrial and business centres. Canada is a member of NAFTA (the North American Free Trade Agreement).

Most Canadians are descended from European settlers, and the two main languages spoken are English and French. A number of French Canadians want Quebec to become an independent nation. Canada also has a growing Asian population. Descendants of the first Canadians, Native Americans and Inuit, today number about 330,000.

The Niagara Falls lie on a strait between Lakes Erie and Ontario, on the Canadian-US border. Two great cascades drop over sheer cliffs in a colossal curtain of spray.

The CN Tower soars to a height of 553 metres above the skyline of Toronto, in Ontario. This lakeside city is the biggest in Canada, a centre of international business and industries such as food-processing, meat-packing, engineering and clothing.

Canada

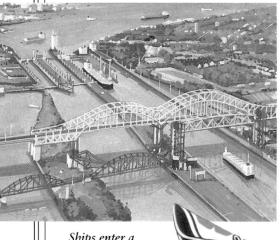

Ships enter a system of locks as they navigate the St Lawrence River and Seaway. This vital link, opened in 1959, gives Atlantic shipping access to the industrial cities of the Great Lakes region. Before the Seaway was built, there were several impassable rapids on the route.

Native American peoples live on the Pacific coast of North America. Tall totem poles of carved wood may be seen in their villages. They feature figures from ancient myths and legends.

ARCTIC OCEAN

Banks Island

ALASKA (U.S.A.)

Porcupine

Dawson

YUKON TERRITORY

Mt. Logan 5959m

★Whitehorse

Great Bear Lake

Mackenzie

Liard

Yellowknife

Great Slave Lake

BRITISH COLUMBIA

Prince Rupert

Peace

Peace River

ALBERTA

Mt. Robson 3954m

Edmonton★

N. Saskatchewan

Rocky Mountains

Fraser

Calgary

Medicine Hat

Saskatoo

Pri Alb

S. Saskatchewan

Vancouver Island

Vancouver

Victoria★

NORTH PACIFIC OCEAN

UNITED STATES

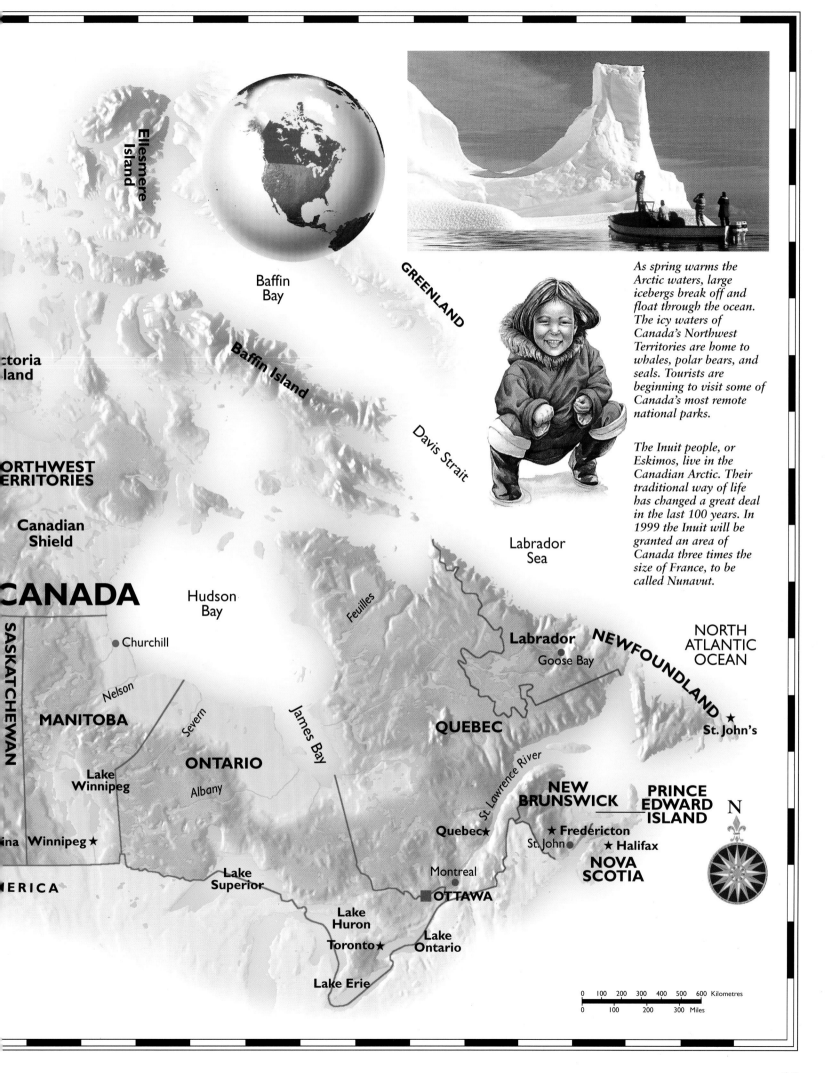

Ellesmere Island

Baffin Bay

GREENLAND

ctoria land

Baffin Island

Davis Strait

NORTHWEST TERRITORIES

Canadian Shield

Labrador Sea

CANADA

Hudson Bay

Feuilles

Labrador

NEWFOUNDLAND

NORTH ATLANTIC OCEAN

Churchill

Goose Bay

SASKATCHEWAN

Nelson

MANITOBA

Severn

James Bay

QUEBEC

St. John's

ONTARIO

Albany

Lake Winnipeg

St. Lawrence River

NEW BRUNSWICK

PRINCE EDWARD ISLAND

N

ina Winnipeg ★

Quebec★

★ Fredericton

St. John ●

★ Halifax

ERICA

Lake Superior

Montreal

NOVA SCOTIA

■ OTTAWA

Lake Huron

Toronto ★

Lake Ontario

Lake Erie

As spring warms the Arctic waters, large icebergs break off and float through the ocean. The icy waters of Canada's Northwest Territories are home to whales, polar bears, and seals. Tourists are beginning to visit some of Canada's most remote national parks.

The Inuit people, or Eskimos, live in the Canadian Arctic. Their traditional way of life has changed a great deal in the last 100 years. In 1999 the Inuit will be granted an area of Canada three times the size of France, to be called Nunavut.

| 0 | 100 | 200 | 300 | 400 | 500 | 600 Kilometres |
| 0 | 100 | | 200 | | 300 Miles | |

United States of America

The United States of America stretches a third of the way around the Earth, crossing eight time zones. It occupies the centre of the North American continent, lying between the North Atlantic and the North Pacific oceans. It also takes in Alaska, far to the north, and the distant Hawaiian islands, in the Pacific Ocean. The USA is divided into 50 states, each one represented by a star on the national flag.

Land and climate vary hugely, encompassing Arctic wilderness, the burning deserts of Arizona, the northern forests and southern swamps, great chains of mountains and the rolling grasslands called prairies. The western state of California lies within an earthquake zone, and the Hawaiian islands have volcanic eruptions. In parts of the USA there are great cities of gleaming skyscrapers and sprawling factories, linked by busy freeways.

The USA is rich in natural resources. It produces aircraft, motor vehicles, electrical goods and computers and is the world leader in business and finance.

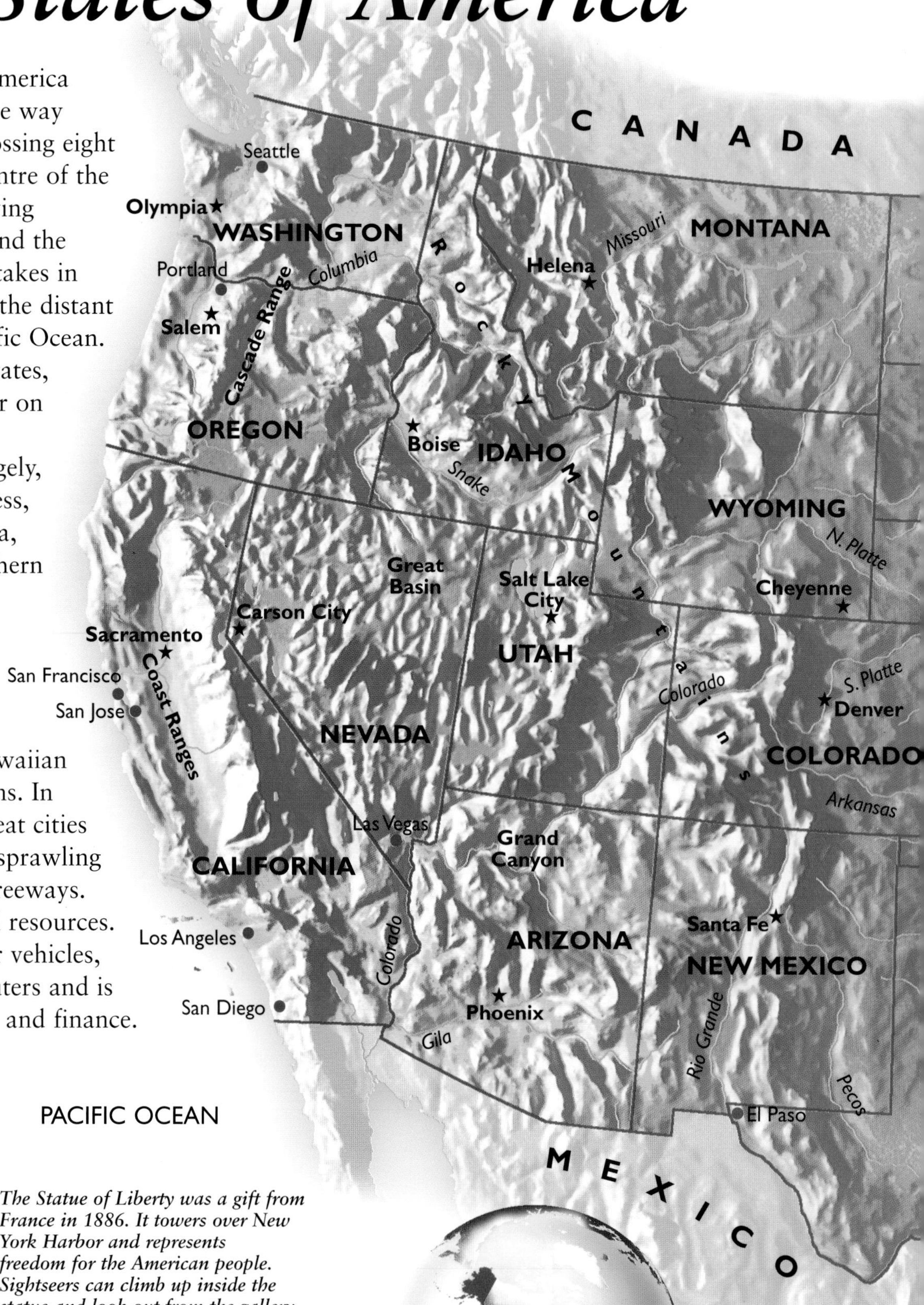

PACIFIC OCEAN

The Statue of Liberty was a gift from France in 1886. It towers over New York Harbor and represents freedom for the American people. Sightseers can climb up inside the statue and look out from the gallery under Liberty's crown.

CANADA

Seattle
Olympia★
WASHINGTON
Portland
Salem★
Columbia
Cascade Range
OREGON
Boise★
IDAHO
Snake
MONTANA
Missouri
Helena★

Rocky

WYOMING
N. Platte
Cheyenne★

Great Basin
Salt Lake City★
UTAH
Carson City★
Sacramento★
San Francisco
San Jose
Coast Ranges
NEVADA

Mountains

Colorado
S. Platte
Denver★
COLORADO
Arkansas

Las Vegas
Grand Canyon

CALIFORNIA

Los Angeles
Colorado
ARIZONA
Santa Fe★
NEW MEXICO

San Diego
Phoenix★
Gila
Rio Grande
Pecos
El Paso

MEXICO

Most North American wild cats live in undeveloped areas west of the Mississippi River. The jaguar was found in the Southwest up until the early 1900s, though now it is restricted to Central and South America.

United States of America

MAINE

VERMONT

★ Augusta

MASSACHUSETTS

Montpelier ★

NEW HAMPSHIRE

Concord ★

Lake Superior

MINNESOTA

ORTH AKOTA

Bismarck

OUTH AKOTA

★ Pierre

Minneapolis

St Paul ★

WISCONSIN

Madison ★

Milwaukee

MICHIGAN

Lake Huron

Lake Michigan

Lansing ★

Detroit

Lake Ontario

Lake Erie

Buffalo

Albany ★

Hartford ★

NEW YORK

★ Boston

RHODE IS.

★ Providence

CONNECTICUT

New York City

Cleveland

PENNSYLVANIA

Harrisburg ★

Pittsburgh

NEW JERSEY

★ Trenton

Philadelphia

Des Moines ★

Chicago

Toledo

OHIO

Columbus ★

Baltimore ●

★ Dover

★ Annapolis

DELAWARE

IOWA

ILLINOIS

INDIANA

Indianapolis ★

Cincinnati

WEST VIRGINIA

WASHINGTON D.C.

MARYLAND

EBRASKA

Lincoln ★

Missouri

Springfield ★

Ohio

Charleston ★

Richmond ★

VIRGINIA

Kansas City

Jefferson City ★

St. Louis

Frankfort ★

KENTUCKY

Winston-Salem ●

NORTH CAROLINA

Topeka ★

KANSAS

MISSOURI

★ Raleigh

OKLAHOMA

Oklahoma City ★

Arkansas

Little Rock ★

ARKANSAS

★ Nashville

TENNESSEE

Memphis ●

Tennessee

SOUTH CAROLINA

★ Columbia

Red River

MISSISSIPPI

Alabama

Atlanta ★

Dallas ●

Brazos

LOUISIANA

Mississippi

Jackson ★

Montgomery ★

ALABAMA

GEORGIA

NORTH ATLANTIC OCEAN

EXAS

Austin ●

Baton Rouge ★

New Orleans

Tallahassee ★

Jacksonville ●

San Antonio ●

Houston ●

Rio Grande

FLORIDA

Gulf of Mexico

● Miami

N

0	100	200	300	400	Kilometres
0	50	100	150	200	250	Miles

Great Plains

Appalachian Mountains

Tens of thousands of years ago, Asia and North America were joined across what is now the Bering Strait. Over the ages, people from Siberia crossed into the Americas and moved southwards. These were the Native Americans, whose descendants still live in the USA today. Europeans – Spanish, French, Dutch and British – began to settle in North America in the 1500s and 1600s. They seized lands from the Native Americans and forced people from Africa to work for the settlers as slaves. The British colonists in the east declared their independence from British rule in 1776, forming a new republic. The new country grew and grew.

Today, many different people live in the USA, including the descendants of Africans, Irish, Italians, Germans, Poles, Jews, Chinese and Japanese. Many of these groups have kept their own traditions, but see themselves as American citizens. The rights of each citizen are guaranteed by the Constitution, which was first drawn up when the country was founded. Some US laws are federal, covering the whole nation; others vary from state to state. The USA is a democracy with two main political parties, the Democrats and the Republicans. Head of state is a President, elected every four years.

ARCTIC OCEAN

RUSSIA

Bering Strait

Bering Sea

ALASKA

Nome
Barrow
Colville
Noatak
Kobuk
Koyukuk
Brooks Range
Porcupine
Fort Yukon
Yukon
CANADA
Fairbanks
Tanana
▲ Mt. McKinley 6194m
Alaska Range
Anchorage
Kenai
Copper
Bethel
Seward
Cordova
Dillingham
Homer
Juneau
Gulf of Alaska
Sitka
Ketchikan
Kodiak

Aleutian Islands

PACIFIC OCEAN

Jambalaya is a spicy hotch-potch of a dish which might include prawns, fish, rice, green peppers and chilli. It comes from New Orleans in Louisiana, a southern city where French influences mix with African-American tastes.

Every autumn, Monarch butterflies from southern Canada and the northern United States migrate southwards to Mexico in huge flocks, returning the following spring.

The bald eagle is the national emblem of the United States. Once common throughout most of North America, this powerful bird of prey became scarce as a result of poisoning by pesticides. Its numbers are now increasing and it is still common in Alaska.

Eastern Woodlands Moccasins and a plains pipe, beautifully hand-crafted by Native Americans. Native Americans lived in North America for many thousands of years before the arrival of the first European settlers.

The White House is the official home of the President of the United States. It is in Washington, D.C. (District of Columbia), the federal capital.

KAUAI
Kapaa
NIIHAU
OAHU
Kaneohe
Honolulu★
MOLOKAI
Kualapuu
Lahaina
LANAI
MAUI
KAHOOLAWE
Mauna Kea 4205m ▲
Hilo
HAWAII
▲ Mauna Loa 4169m

Eastern and southern states

The eastern seaboard of the United States stretches from the stormy, rocky shores of Maine down to the sunny sandbanks and islands of the Florida Keys. Inland, the long, wooded spine of the Appalachian Mountains runs north to south. To the west, the continent is crossed by the vast Mississippi-Missouri river system. This flows into the Gulf of Mexico, a warm, shallow sea fringed by swamps and steamy creeks, called bayous. The huge, dry state of Texas is cattle-ranching country.

The eastern part of the USA was the first to be settled by Europeans and the first to build big industrial cities. A bitter civil war was fought between northern and southern states between 1861 and 1865.

Times Square is on Manhattan Island in New York City. It lies at the heart of New York's theatre district, and its bright lights advertise shows, musicals, plays and films.

A white church spire rises against the autumn tints of woodland in Vermont, one of the six northeastern states which together make up the region known as New England. This is an area of green, wooded hills and rocky shores.

A space shuttle blasts off from the John F. Kennedy Space Center at Cape Canaveral in Florida, hitching a ride on powerful rockets. The USA has been a leading pioneer in space exploration. The shuttles have been used to launch satellites and to carry out scientific experiments in space. Following their mission they can land like aircraft.

State	Popular name	Capital	Bird	Flower	Tree
Alabama	Camellia State	Montgomery	Yellowhammer	Camellia	Southern Pine
Arkansas	Land of Opportunity	Little Rock	Mockingbird	Apple blossom	Pine
Connecticut	Constitution State	Hartford	Robin	Mountain laurel	White oak
Delaware	First State	Dover	Blue hen chicken	Peach blossom	American holly
Florida	Sunshine State	Tallahassee	Mockingbird	Orange blossom	Palmetto palm
Georgia	Empire State of the South	Atlanta	Brown thrasher	Cherokee rose	Live oak
Kentucky	Bluegrass State	Frankfort	Kentucky cardinal	Goldenrod	Tulip poplar
Louisiana	Pelican State	Baton Rouge	Brown pelican	Magnolia	Bald cypress
Maine	Pine Tree State	Augusta	Chickadee	White pine cone and tassel	White pine
Maryland	Old Line State	Annapolis	Baltimore oriole	Black-eyed susan	White oak
Massachusetts	Bay State	Boston	Chickadee	Mayflower	American elm
Mississippi	Magnolia State	Jackson	Mockingbird	Magnolia	Magnolia
New Hampshire	Granite State	Concord	Purple finch	Purple lilac	White birch
New Jersey	Garden State	Trenton	Eastern goldfinch	Purple violet	Red oak
New York	Empire State	Albany	Bluebird	Rose	Sugar maple
North Carolina	Tar Heel State	Raleigh	Cardinal	Flowering dogwood	Pine
Oklahoma	Sooner State	Oklahoma City	Scissor-tailed flycatcher	Mistletoe	Redbud
Pennsylvania	Keystone State	Harrisburg	Ruffed grouse	Mountain laurel	Hemlock
Rhode Island	Little Rhody	Providence	Rhode Island red	Violet	Red maple
South Carolina	Palmetto State	Columbia	Carolina wren	Yellow jessamine	Palmetto
Tennessee	Volunteer State	Nashville	Mockingbird	Iris	Tulip poplar
Texas	Lone Star State	Austin	Mockingbird	Blue bonnet	Pecan
Vermont	Green Mountain State	Montpelier	Hermit thrush	Red clover	Sugar maple
Virginia	Old Dominion	Richmond	Cardinal	Flowering dogwood	Dogwood
West Virginia	Mountain State	Charleston	Cardinal	Rhododendron	Sugar maple

The United States Congress meets at the Capitol in Washington D.C. The USA is a democracy. Its two largest political parties are the Republicans and the Democrats.

The colour and magical atmosphere of Walt Disney's cartoons are reflected in the huge Disney theme parks in California and Florida.

Between 1927 and 1941 the faces of four US presidents were carved in the rockface at Mount Rushmore in South Dakota. The portraits are of George Washington, Thomas Jefferson, Theodore Roosevelt and Abraham Lincoln. The heads, 142 metres high, are a monument to democracy.

Ninety-five percent of the state of Iowa is taken up by farmland, and most of that is given over to crops such as soya beans, maize, wheat, rye and flax.

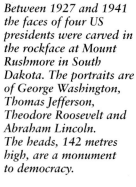

The Midwest

America's 'Midwest' stretches from the Central Lowlands around the Missouri River, westwards across the High Plains to the foothills of the Rocky Mountains. Once the home of Native American buffalo-hunters, these fertile grasslands were settled by European Americans during the 1800s. The prairie grasses are taller in the wetter eastern states than in the dry shadow of the Rockies. Crops include maize and wheat, while shortgrass regions are grazed by large herds of cattle, or by bison which are now protected by law. Sometimes tornadoes spin across the farmland, raising tall columns of dust. During the 1930s changes in land use and lack of rain caused large areas of farmland to become a great dustbowl. Many farmers had to give up their life on the land. Today, the prairie lands are protected from the wind by plantations of trees and are carefully conserved. There are still areas of wild prairie, many within National Park areas.

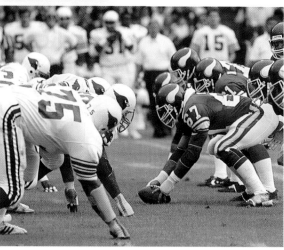

American football is a popular sport in colleges and stadiums right across the USA. Players wear helmets and heavy padding for this tough, fast, contact sport which is attracting many followers in other countries.

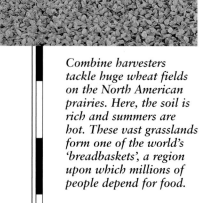

Combine harvesters tackle huge wheat fields on the North American prairies. Here, the soil is rich and summers are hot. These vast grasslands form one of the world's 'breadbaskets', a region upon which millions of people depend for food.

State	Popular name	Capital	Bird	Flower	Tree
Illinois	Prairie State	Springfield	Cardinal	Violet	White oak
Indiana	Hoosier State	Indianapolis	Cardinal	Peony	Tulip poplar
Iowa	Hawkeye State	Des Moines	Eastern goldfinch	Wild rose	Oak
Kansas	Sunflower State	Topeka	Western meadowlark	Sunflower	Cottonwood
Michigan	Wolverine State	Lansing	Robin	Apple blossom	White pine
Minnesota	Gopher State	St Paul	Common loon	Pink and white lady's slipper	Norway or red pine
Missouri	Show Me State	Jefferson City	Bluebird	Hawthorn	Flowering dogwood
Nebraska	Cornhusker State	Lincoln	Western meadowlark	Goldenrod	American elm
North Dakota	Flickertail State	Bismarck	Western meadowlark	Wild prairie rose	Cottonwood
Ohio	Buckeye State	Columbus	Cardinal	Scarlet carnation	Buckeye
South Dakota	Mt Rushmore State	Pierre	Ring-necked pheasant	Pasqueflower	Black Hills spruce
Wisconsin	Badger State	Madison	Robin	Wood violet	Sugar maple

The Grand Canyon is the biggest gorge to be found on any continent. It is about 16 kilometres wide and about 1.5 kilometres deep. It has been carved from the rocks of Arizona by the waters of the Colorado River. The area is a National Park.

Western and mountain states

The Rocky Mountains form a great chain, running through Canada and the United States down to Mexico. To the west of them lies a strangely beautiful landscape of salt flats, deserts, eroded rocks and canyons. These dry lands lie in the shadow of further mountain barriers, the Sierra Nevada and the Cascade and Coast ranges. The western slopes of these mountains catch incoming Pacific rains.

The west coast enjoys a mild climate. California is warm and sunny, while Oregon and Washington are cooler and wetter. Big cities include Seattle, San Francisco and Los Angeles, where the Hollywood district is the centre of the film industry. The region is an earthquake danger zone, and serious tremors have caused damage to Californian cities over the last 100 years.

Alaska and the Rocky Mountains are the haunt of various species of bear. The polar bear is the largest flesh-eating animal, and the Kodiak brown bear is also huge and fierce.

Grizzly bear

North American black bear

Kodiak brown bear

Polar bear

Bizarre tufa towers rim the shores of Mono Lake in California. They form when calcium in fresh water reacts with the lake water, which is three times saltier than the Pacific. The towers used to be underwater until the lake's water supply was diverted to Los Angeles and the lake became half as full.

Compact discs, microprocessors and other high-technology electronic goods are produced in California. One part of the state has been nicknamed 'Silicon Valley'.

Old-fashioned cable cars are a favourite sight in San Francisco. This large port, built on hills around a beautiful bay, includes wooden houses from 100 years ago as well as modern, earthquake-proof skyscrapers.

State	Popular name	Capital	Bird	Flower	Tree
Alaska	Last Frontier	Juneau	Willow ptarmigan	Forget-me-not	Sitka spruce
Arizona	Grand Canyon State	Phoenix	Cactus wren	Saguaro	Paloverde
California	Golden State	Sacramento	California valley quail	Golden poppy	California redwood
Colorado	Centennial State	Denver	Lark bunting	Rocky Mt columbine	Blue spruce
Hawaii	Aloha State	Honolulu	Nene (Hawaiian goose)	Hibiscus	Kukui (Candlenut)
Idaho	Gem state	Boise	Mountain bluebird	Syringa	Western white pine
Montana	Treasure State	Helena	Western meadowlark	Bitterroot	Ponderosa pine
Nevada	Silver State	Carson City	Mountain bluebird	Sagebrush	Single-leaf piñon
New Mexico	Land of Enchantment	Santa Fe	Roadrunner	Yucca	Piñon
Oregon	Beaver State	Salem	Western meadowlark	Oregon grape	Douglas fir
Utah	Beehive State	Salt Lake City	Seagull	Sego lily	Blue spruce
Washington	Evergreen State	Olympia	Willow goldfinch	Western rhododendron	Western hemlock
Wyoming	Equality State	Cheyenne	Meadowlark	Indian paintbrush	Cottonwood

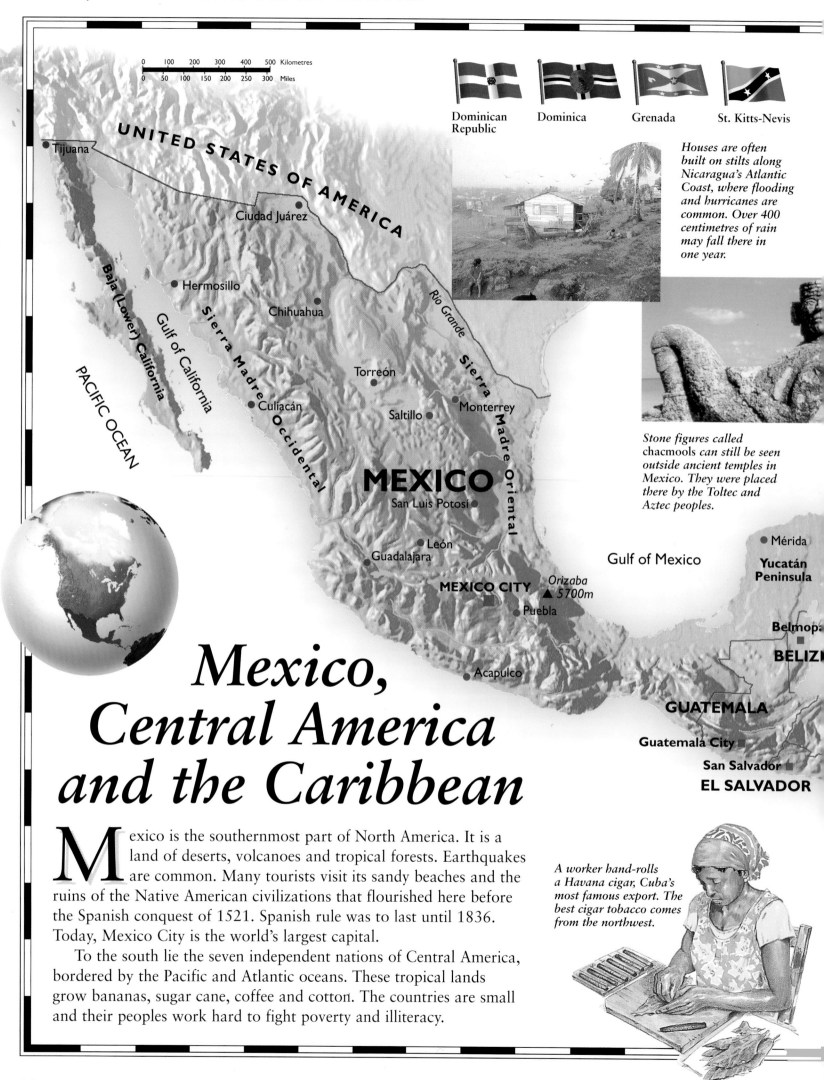

0 100 200 300 400 500 Kilometres
0 50 100 150 200 250 300 Miles

Dominican Republic

Dominica

Grenada

St. Kitts-Nevis

Houses are often built on stilts along Nicaragua's Atlantic Coast, where flooding and hurricanes are common. Over 400 centimetres of rain may fall there in one year.

UNITED STATES OF AMERICA

Tijuana

Ciudad Juárez

Hermosillo

Chihuahua

Baja (Lower) California

Gulf of California

Sierra Madre Occidental

PACIFIC OCEAN

Torreón

Culiacán

Saltillo

Monterrey

Río Grande

Sierra Madre Oriental

MEXICO

San Luis Potosí

Stone figures called chacmools *can still be seen outside ancient temples in Mexico. They were placed there by the Toltec and Aztec peoples.*

León

Guadalajara

MEXICO CITY

Orizaba ▲ 5700m

Puebla

Gulf of Mexico

Mérida

Yucatán Peninsula

Acapulco

Belmopa

BELIZ

GUATEMALA

Guatemala City

San Salvador

EL SALVADOR

Mexico, Central America and the Caribbean

Mexico is the southernmost part of North America. It is a land of deserts, volcanoes and tropical forests. Earthquakes are common. Many tourists visit its sandy beaches and the ruins of the Native American civilizations that flourished here before the Spanish conquest of 1521. Spanish rule was to last until 1836. Today, Mexico City is the world's largest capital.

To the south lie the seven independent nations of Central America, bordered by the Pacific and Atlantic oceans. These tropical lands grow bananas, sugar cane, coffee and cotton. The countries are small and their peoples work hard to fight poverty and illiteracy.

A worker hand-rolls a Havana cigar, Cuba's most famous export. The best cigar tobacco comes from the northwest.

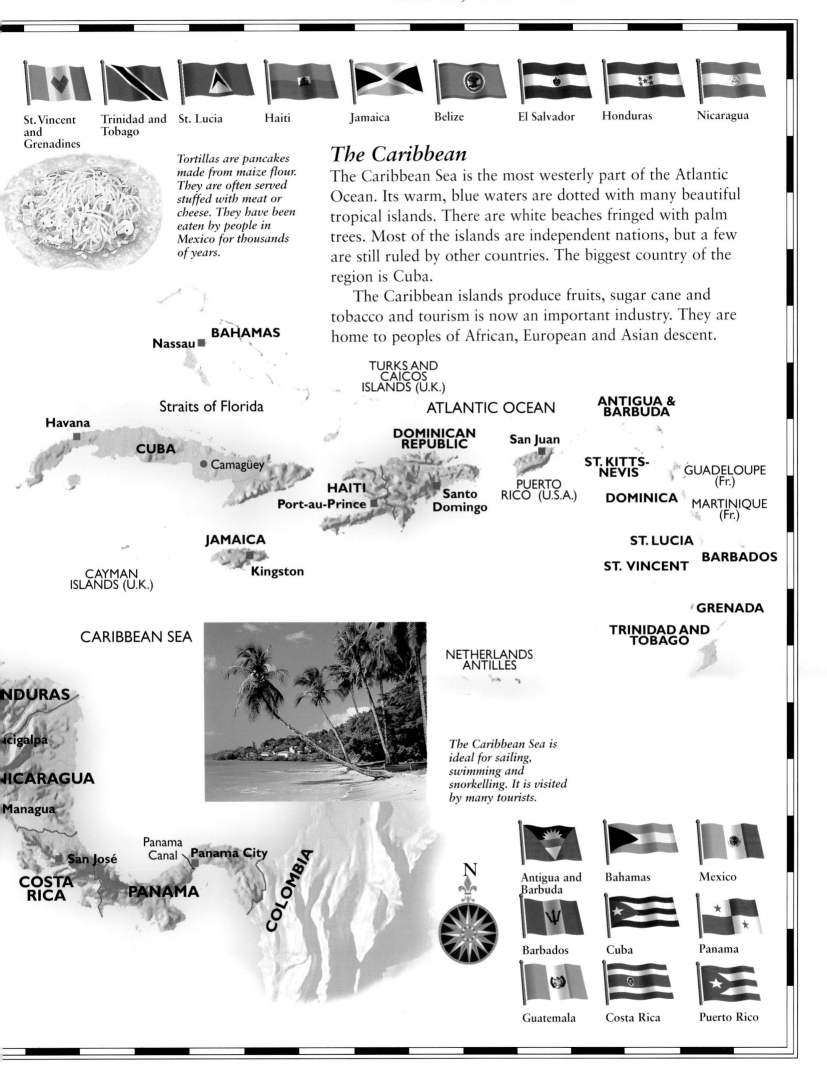

St. Vincent and Grenadines

Trinidad and Tobago

St. Lucia

Haiti

Jamaica

Belize

El Salvador

Honduras

Nicaragua

Tortillas are pancakes made from maize flour. They are often served stuffed with meat or cheese. They have been eaten by people in Mexico for thousands of years.

The Caribbean

The Caribbean Sea is the most westerly part of the Atlantic Ocean. Its warm, blue waters are dotted with many beautiful tropical islands. There are white beaches fringed with palm trees. Most of the islands are independent nations, but a few are still ruled by other countries. The biggest country of the region is Cuba.

The Caribbean islands produce fruits, sugar cane and tobacco and tourism is now an important industry. They are home to peoples of African, European and Asian descent.

Nassau ■ **BAHAMAS**

TURKS AND CAICOS ISLANDS (U.K.)

Straits of Florida

ATLANTIC OCEAN

ANTIGUA & BARBUDA

Havana ■

CUBA

● Camagüey

DOMINICAN REPUBLIC

San Juan

ST. KITTS- NEVIS

GUADELOUPE (Fr.)

HAITI
Port-au-Prince ■

Santo Domingo

PUERTO RICO (U.S.A.)

DOMINICA

MARTINIQUE (Fr.)

JAMAICA

■ **Kingston**

ST. LUCIA

ST. VINCENT

BARBADOS

CAYMAN ISLANDS (U.K.)

GRENADA

TRINIDAD AND TOBAGO

CARIBBEAN SEA

NETHERLANDS ANTILLES

The Caribbean Sea is ideal for sailing, swimming and snorkelling. It is visited by many tourists.

NDURAS

cigalpa

NICARAGUA

Managua

Panama Canal

Panama City ■

COLOMBIA

San José

COSTA RICA

PANAMA

N

Antigua and Barbuda

Bahamas

Mexico

Barbados

Cuba

Panama

Guatemala

Costa Rica

Puerto Rico

The Northern Andes

The western part of South America is dominated by a long mountain chain called the Andes, which runs for 6,400 kilometres from north to south. In Ecuador alone there are 18 peaks rising more than 4,500 metres above sea level. To the west of the Andes, a narrow coastal plain borders the Pacific Ocean. To the east, rivers drain into the vast rainforests of the Amazon basin.

This part of South America saw the rise of great civilizations such as the Chimú and the Inca, before the arrival of Spanish invaders in the 1530s. The region broke away from Spanish rule during the 1820s and today makes up four independent nations – Colombia, Ecuador, Peru and Bolivia.

Many Indians, such as the Aymara and the Quechua, still live in these countries. Other inhabitants are of European or mixed descent, and Spanish is spoken throughout the region.

The area is rich in mineral resources and timber, but many people work for very low wages. Crops include maize, sugar cane, bananas, coffee, potatoes, and a grain called quinoa.

The Andean countries are famous for their finely woven blankets, ponchos and belts. These are woven on back-strap looms, using methods that have changed little since Inca times.

These women are from La Paz, in Bolivia. La Paz is the world's highest capital city, sited at 3,684 metres above sea level in the Andes range. The city is a centre of trading in fine alpaca wool. In the cool mountain climate, these women wear woollen shawls and felt hats.

The Sun played an important role in the religion of the Incas, as this Inca Sun Festival at Sascayhuaman in Cuzco shows. The first Inca emperor was believed to be a descendant of the Sun.

This antique gold cross is studded with emeralds. Raw emeralds are found in the Andes. Huge emeralds weighing as much as 7.4 kg have been found in Colombia. They then have to be cut in a special way to make them sparkle.

Machu Picchu was just one town in the powerful Inca empire, which flourished about 500 years ago. Its ruins were discovered in 1911, high in the Peruvian Andes. The Incas were expert builders, engineers, farmers, and craft workers. Machu Picchu included temples and a palace. Its aqueduct channelled fresh water into the town.

Sure-footed alpacas are used to carry goods high in the Andes mountains. Alpacas also provide meat and hides and their wool may be spun and woven.

This is one of over 300 statues that have been found in the hills near San Augustin in Colombia. They are at least 1,000 years old and seem to mark burial sites. Colombia was originally home to many groups of Indians, some living in rainforest settlements, others wandering the open plains. Another group, the Chibcha in the Andes, made beautiful jewellery and ornaments.

Colombia

Ecuador

Peru

Bolivia

N

Reed boats are used on Titicaca, the world's highest navigable lake. It is over 3,800 metres above sea level, on the border between Bolivia and Peru, and covers an area of 8,288 square kilometres. The area around the lake is the homeland of the Aymara, an Indian tribe. The Aymara catch fish such as orestias and trout from the deep, cold waters of a lake.

Indians make up over half the population of Ecuador. This Waorani hunter is from the rainforest region. He hunts animals by shooting poison-tipped darts through a blow-pipe.

Popular musical instruments of the Andes include the **rondador** (pan-pipes), flutes, drums and guitars. The music is influenced by both Spanish and Indian traditions. Performers often wear regional costume.

Caribbean Sea

TRINIDAD
AND TOBAGO

Caracas

Maracaibo

Orinoco

COLOMBIA

VENEZUELA

Georgetown

Paramaribo

GUYANA
SURINAME

Cayenne

FRENCH
GUIANA

Orinoco

Guiana Highlands

Branco

Negro

Japurá

Manaus

Amazon

Macapá

Belèm

ATLANTIC
OCEAN

Amazon

Tocantins

Fortaleza

PERU

Juruá

Purus

Madeira

Tapajós

Xingu

Araguaia

Parnaíba

São Francisco

Recife

Guaporé

BOLIVIA

BRAZIL

Brazilian
Highlands

Salvador

Mato Grosso
Plateau

BRASÍLIA

Goiânia

PARAGUAY

Paraná

Belo Horizonte

Rio de Janeiro

São Paulo

Iguaçu
Falls

Curitiba

ARGENTINA

Uruguay

URUGUAY

Pôrto Alegre

Flags:

Brazil

Guyana

Suriname

French Guiana

Venezuela

Many Indians lived in
South America at the
time it was conquered by
Spain and Portugal.
However many were
killed or enslaved. Today,
proud of their traditions,
the Indian tribes struggle
to survive and keep their
own lands.

The Kamayura are an
Indian people who live in
the Amazonian
rainforest. The men wear
feather headdresses, face
paint and earplugs.

Many people in Suriname
are the descendants of
workers from Java, in
southeast Asia. They
came to Suriname during
the years when it was
ruled by the Dutch. Here
they are performing a
traditional folk dance.

Brazil and its neighbours

A statue in Caracas, Venezuela, honours the revolutionary hero Simón Bolívar (1783-1830). Bolívar fought for independence from Spain in the 1800s. He campaigned in Venezuela, Colombia, Peru, Ecuador and Bolivia trying to create a federation of Spanish-speaking nations.

Brazil is the largest country in South America. It is crossed by the mighty river Amazon and a vast area of it is covered by rainforest, whose wealth of plants and wildlife is threatened as millions of trees are cut down to make way for farms and roads. Brazil also takes in grasslands and dry scrub.

To the north, Venezuela stretches from the marshes and lakes of the coast to the humid rain forests that cover the mountains in the west and south. The River Orinoco winds through the centre of the country, and the grasslands of the Llanos are often flooded. Three small countries – Guyana, Surinam and French Guiana – also lie between the highlands and the Caribbean coast.

The whole region was colonized by the Portuguese, Spanish, Dutch, British and French from the 1500s onwards. Today it is home to many different Indian tribes although most people are of European, African and Asian descent.

Crops include sugar-cane and coffee, and the region has many natural resources. Oil brings wealth to Venezuela, and Brazil is rich in minerals. However, many people are very poor and live in home-made shacks around growing cities such as Rio de Janeiro. Brazil is famous for its fine beaches, its carnival dances and its love of soccer.

The red chilli pod is used to make Cayenne pepper, a fiery spice named after the capital of French Guiana. This is the only country in the region that is not yet independent, being an overseas department of France. French Guiana relies on its crops, but also has reserves of timber, gold and bauxite.

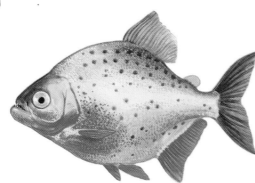

Piranha fish live in many South American rivers. They have razor-sharp teeth which can rip the flesh from any animal that falls into the water in just a few seconds. Piranha fish swim in shoals numbering thousands. There are 18 species of piranha.

At Christmas in Venezuela, you may be offered halacas. Stewed meats are put inside a pastry case made of cornflour. This is wrapped in plantain leaves and cooked in boiling water. It is usually eaten with ham and bread.

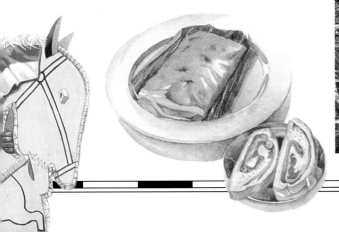

The statue of Christ, on Corcovado peak, towers above the beautiful city and fine, natural harbour of Rio de Janeiro in Brazil.

The threatened rainforests of the tropical Amazonian Basin are a wonder of the world. Numerous species of tree, fern and creeper grow here and they are populated with monkeys, sloths, parrots, huge snakes and countless insects.

Southern South America

The jagged peaks of the Andes range continue southwards through the long, narrow country of Chile. This beautiful land includes one of the driest regions on Earth, the Atacama desert on the northern coast. The southern coastline is ragged, breaking up into a maze of islands.

Paraguay lies at the heart of the continent, a hot, humid country. In its west are the thinly populated plains of the Gran Chaco, in the east are forest and grassland zones. Uruguay lies on South America's Atlantic coast above the broad estuary of the Rio de la Plata or River Plate. Its huge southern neighbour, Argentina, takes in the wide open grasslands of the Pampa. To the south lies the bleak plateau of Patagonia and Tierra del Fuego, a cold, desolate island shared with Chile.

The varied climate of southern South America means that regional produce includes very different items, such as potatoes, citrus fruits, olives, wines, sugar cane, rice and coffee. Argentina is a major producer of beef and is famed for its cattle-ranching and its cowboys, or gauchos. Fishing is a major industry in the southern oceans. Factories manufacture cars, electrical goods and textiles. Far out in the south Atlantic Ocean are two British territories, the Malvinas, or Falkland Islands, and the more remote islands of South Georgia. Argentina went to war with Britain over ownership of the islands in 1982-83.

Buenos Aires is the capital of Argentina. It is large city and seaport on the west bank of the Plate estuary. Its name means 'favourable winds'.

Punta Arenas exports locally produced wool and lamb. This seaport lies in the remote south of Chile, on the Strait of Magellan. The strait provides a sea route between the Pacific and Atlantic oceans.

A statue in Montevideo commemorates the early Spanish settlers who came to build farms and ranches, crossing the land with ox-carts. Later immigrants to southern South America included Italians, Welsh, Germans, Dutch, Poles, Hungarians and Lebanese.

The ruined church of San Ignacio is in the province of Misiones, in north-eastern Argentina. The province is named after the Jesuit missionaries who came to the region in the 1600s, with the aim of bringing Christianity to the Guaraní people.

Native American peoples living in the southern half of the continent include the Guaraní, the Mataco and the Mapuche. The arrival of the first European settlers brought war and disease to many indigenous peoples.

This bedspread is being made out of a fine lace, known to the Guaraní people of Paraguay as ñanduti, or 'spider's web'. The patterns include designs of flowers, birds and animals.

PERU

Arica

Iquique

BOLIVIA

Atacama Desert

PARAGUAY

Antofagasta

Gran Chaco

BRAZIL

Asunción

CHILE

Tucumán

Salado

Paraná

Uruguay

ARGENTINA

Córdoba

Rosario

URUGUAY

Valparaíso

▲ Aconcagua 6959m

Montevideo

Santiago

BUENOS AIRES

Concepción

Pampas

Mar del Plata

Colorado

Bahia Blanca

Negro

Andes

PATAGONIA

Chubut

SOUTH ATLANTIC OCEAN

N

FALKLAND ISLANDS (U.K.)

Tierra del Fuego

SOUTH GEORGIA (U.K.)

Cape Horn

| 0 | 25 | 50 | 75 | Kilometres |
| 0 | 10 | 20 | 30 | 40 | 50 | Miles |

Argentina

Chile

Paraguay

Uruguay

Maté is a hot, bitter drink that is popular in South America. It is rather like tea, but is brewed from the leaves of a type of holly that grows in Paraguay. Traditionally it is drunk through a tube from a hollow gourd.

The Congress building in Buenos Aires. Argentina today is a democracy, but like many other South American countries, it has gone through long periods of dictatorship, military rule and political unrest since it became independent from Spain in 1816.

Scandinavia and Finland

Two claw-shaped peninsulas jut out from northern Europe. The larger one stretches south from the Arctic and takes in Sweden and Norway. It includes mountains, sea inlets called fjords, lakes and forests. The smaller peninsula, an area of green farmland, extends northwards from Germany. Together with various islands, this makes up Denmark. The whole region is called Scandinavia. Far to the west, in the Atlantic Ocean, is the bleak island of Iceland, which is partly covered by icefields and glaciers. Iceland was settled by Scandinavian seafarers called Vikings in AD 874. To the east, across the Gulf of Bothnia, the lakes and forests of Finland stretch to the Russian border.

Swedes, Norwegians, Danes and Icelanders are all closely related, and so are the languages they speak. The Finns speak a very different language, as do the Saami or Lapps, a people who live in the far north.

The region is rich in natural resources such as timber, iron ore, and offshore oil and gas from the North Sea. The Icelandic economy depends on catching and processing fish. Iceland also uses energy from its volcanic rocks to heat greenhouses for garden produce. Sweden, Denmark and Finland are members of the European Union.

Danish pastries are delicious, sweet rolls and twists, which are often iced and filled with raisins or other fruit. They are eaten mid-morning, with cups of strong coffee.

In winter the Swedish countryside is covered in snow and temperatures drop below zero. Summers are warm but brief. This landscape lies near Uddevalla in the southwest, which enjoys a milder climate than the east of the country.

Fish are dried on the Norwegian coast. The Scandinavian countries are almost surrounded by sea. Fishing is a major industry, and Scandinavian cooking includes many recipes for herring or cod.

The towers and gables of Egeskov Castle are reflected in the still waters of the lake. This fortress was built in 1554 on the island of Fyn, in southern Denmark. At that time Denmark and Norway were still united, but Sweden had already broken away from the union. These were troubled times in Danish history. Today the castle serves as a tourist attraction and includes a transport museum.

Isafjördur
Vatneyri
Hólmavík
Bordeyri
Húsavík
Saudárkrókur
Akureyri
Seydisfjördur

ICELAND
Vatnajökull

Akranes
REYKJAVIK
Keflavík
▲ *Oraefajökull* 2119m

Vestmannaeyjar

ARCTIC OCEAN

Finland

Denmark

Iceland

Norway

Sweden

NORTH ATLANTIC
OCEAN

Hammerfest

Vadsø

Kirkenes

Tromsø

▲ *Mount Haltia*
1324m

L a p l a n d

0   50   100   150   200   250   Kilometres
0   50   100   150   Miles

N

Narvik

Kebnekaise
▲ *2111m*

Sodankylä

Svolvær

Kiruna

Bodø

Rovaniemi

Övertorneå

Kemi

Mosjøen

Skellefte

Luleå

Storuman

Ume

Skellefteå

Oulu

Kuopio

Kristiansund

Trondheim

SWEDEN

Umeå

Kokkola

Joensuu

Ostersund

Vaasa

Ålesund

Kaskö

Jyväskylä

Galdhøpiggen
▲ *2469m*

Sundsvall

FINLAND

NORWAY

Särna

Tampere

Lillehammer

Västerdal

Lahti

Bergen

Gävle

Turku

HELSINKI

Aland
Is.

OSLO

Uppsala

Gulf of Finland

Karlstad

Örebro

STOCKHOLM

Stavanger

Skien

Lake
Vänern

ESTONIA

Kristiansand

Baltic Sea

Linköping

Skagerrak

Göteborg

Borås

Västervik

Kattegat

Gotland

Aalborg

Borgholm

DENMARK

Århus

Karlskrona

Esbjerg

COPENHAGEN

Kristianstad

Odense

Malmö

GERMANY

Gulf of Bothnia

RUSSIA

*Lapps in traditional
costume gather outside a
stave church in northern
Norway, a part of the
country known as Lapland.
Many of these wooden
churches date from the
time of the Vikings.*

Netherlands, Belgium &

Netherlands means 'lowlands' and much of this country lies below the level of the North Sea. Over the ages Dutch engineers became experts at flood control and at reclaiming land from the sea. The flat Dutch farmland is crossed by canals and rivers. The Dutch were also great seafarers and during the 1600s their overseas trade brought wealth to cities such as Amsterdam. Today the Netherlands is famous for its electrical and chemical industries, dairy products, vegetables and flowers. Rotterdam is the world's largest seaport.

Neighbouring Belgium is mostly flat, but to the south the land rises to the hills of the Ardennes. Belgium is heavily industrialized, producing steel, chemicals and electronics. Its textile industry dates back to the Middle Ages. Tiny Luxembourg, set amidst rolling farmland and woods, is one of the wealthiest nations in Europe being a world centre of banking.

All three countries have strong historical and economic ties and together helped to set up the European Economic Community (today's European Union) in the 1950s. The region is home to Frisians, Dutch, the closely related Flemings of Belgium, Walloons (French-speaking Belgians), Luxemburgers (who speak a dialect called Letzebuergesch), people of Asian and African descent and other European nationals.

The Netherlands are often referred to as 'Holland', which is really just the name of the region.

A Belgian worker makes fine chocolates by hand. Belgium is famous throughout Europe for excellent chocolate, delicious Ardennes pâtés and meats, fried potatoes and strong beers. Home-grown food crops include wheat, barley, oats, rye, potatoes and sugar beet. However, the Belgian economy today depends more on its efficient factories and businesses than on its traditional farming produce.

The Pond bat is found in this part of Europe, although it is becoming increasingly scarce. It likes to live on marshy lowlands. It hunts by night, swooping over ponds and ditches in search of water insects.

Large, round Dutch cheeses are laid out at Alkmaar near Amsterdam in the Netherlands. Mild Dutch cheeses such as Edam and Gouda are an important export. The Dutch themselves prefer the stronger tasting farmhouse cheeses.

In spring tourists come from around the world to see the windmills and the fields of brightly coloured tulips. Bulbs and seeds for flowers is an important business. The windmills were originally built for controlling the water level.

The Atomium monument in Brussels was built for the 1958 World's Fair as a modern symbol of science and progress. Brussels today is not only the capital of Belgium but is also the headquarters of many European Union institutions, such as the European Parliament, Commission and Monetary System, as well as NATO.

Luxembourg City rises above the river Alzette. It is an important centre of business and is the seat of the European Court of Justice. It has the palace of the Grand Dukes and a fine cathedral.

Luxembourg

The valley of the river Moselle, which forms Luxembourg's southwestern border, is famous for its vineyards. The grapes, grown on steep, sunny terraces, produce fine white wines. The grapes are harvested in early autumn.

Netherlands

Belgium

Luxembourg

N

West Frisian Islands

Waddenzee

Leeuwarden

Groningen

IJsselmeer

AMSTERDAM ■

Enschede

●Leiden

NETHERLANDS

●The Hague

Lek

● Arnhem

● Rotterdam

Maas

Nijmegen

● Breda

● Tilburg

● Eindhoven

G E R M A N Y

● Antwerp

● Ostend

Bruges

Ghent

Leie

Schelde

■ **BRUSSELS**

Maastricht

BELGIUM

● Liège

The Belgians have street parades every year in which people dress up in gigantic costumes. Each costume has a peephole, so the person inside can see where he or she is going.

● Mons

● Namur

Meuse

Botrange 694m ▲

● Charleroi

Sambre

Ardennes Mts.

F R A N C E

Bastogne ●

LUXEMBOURG

■ **LUXEMBOURG**

0 10 20 30 40 50 60 Kilometres
0   10   20   30   40 Miles

The British Isles

The British Isles lie in shallow waters off the coast of northwestern Europe. They are bordered to the west by the Atlantic Ocean. The climate is mild and western shores receive a heavy rainfall, making the fields green.

There are about 5,000 islands, many of them very small. The two largest ones are Great Britain and Ireland. Great Britain is made up of three countries called England, Scotland and Wales, which together form the United Kingdom. The northern part of Ireland is governed by the United Kingdom, but most of Ireland forms a separate, independent republic. Both the United Kingdom and the Irish Republic are members of the European Union. The Isle of Man and the Channel Islands have self-government, but still have close ties with the United Kingdom. Peoples of the British Isles include English, Irish, Scots, Welsh, Jews, Roma (Gypsies), Asians and Afro-Caribbeans.

The British Isles include areas of rich farmland for growing crops and for raising cattle and sheep. The world's first big factories were built here in the 1800s, when Britain was the centre of a worldwide empire. There are still many big cities. More people now work providing services such as banking than in heavy industries.

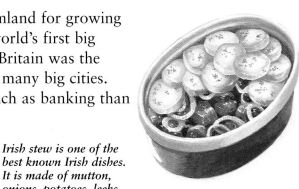

The hardy Highland cattle, with their long shaggy coats, were bred for the harsh climate of the Scottish mountains. The Highland region, a stronghold of ancient Gaelic traditions and language, lives by farming, fishing, forestry and tourism.

Tenby, known in the Welsh language as Dinbych y Pysgod, is in southern Wales. The beautiful western shores of the British Isles are always popular with holiday makers.

Horses are sold at this fair in the town of Drimoleague in the Irish Republic. The Irish countryside is famous for breeding horses for the farm and the race track.

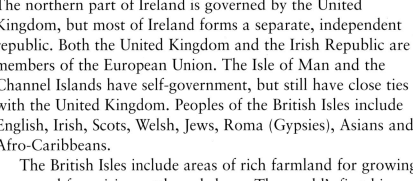

Irish stew is one of the best known Irish dishes. It is made of mutton, onions, potatoes, leeks and carrots, and is served with dumplings.

Saint Paul's is one of the finest cathedrals in England. Lying at the heart of London, it was rebuilt between 1675 and 1710 by an architect called Sir Christopher Wren.

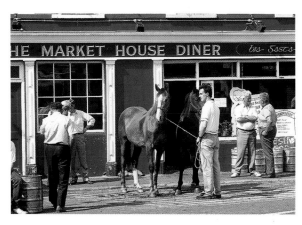

This barrier to the east of London is designed to prevent the River Thames flooding the capital city during North Sea gales. Completed in 1984, its concrete piers support ten steel gates. Normally the gates lie on the river bottom. When tides rise above normal levels, the gates revolve upwards.

United
Kingdom

Ireland

Orkney Is. • Kirkwall

• Thurso

Shetland Is.

• Lerwick

• Stornoway

**Outer
Hebrides**

North West Highlands

Skye

**Loch
Ness** • Inverness

• Peterhead

SCOTLAND

• Aberdeen

ATLANTIC OCEAN

• Mallaig

**Grampian
Highlands**

▲ *Ben Nevis
1343m* *Tay*

N

North Sea

• Oban

• Perth • Dundee

Glasgow •

■ **Edinburgh**

Clyde

Southern Uplands

• Ayr

Tweed

Londonderry

**NORTHERN
IRELAND** ■ **Belfast**

• Stranraer

• Newcastle

Tyne

• Durham

• Sligo

• Armagh

• Carlisle

**Lake
District**

Pennines

• Middlesbrough

IRELAND

• Dundalk

Irish Sea

**Isle of
Man**

Swale

• Blackpool

• Leeds

• Kingston-upon-Hull

• Galway

• Athlone

Liffey ■ **DUBLIN**

• Bradford
Manchester •

• Sheffield

• Liverpool

ENGLAND

Shannon

• Carlow

Wrexham •

• Nottingham

• Derby

• Limerick

• Tipperary

**Cambrian
Mts**

Wolverhampton •

Trent

• Peterborough

• Norwich

• Aberystwyth

Birmingham •

Severn

• Coventry

• Cambridge

Carrauntoohill ▲
1041m

• Killarney

• Waterford

WALES

Wye

• Northampton

• Ipswich

• Cork

Carmarthen •

• Luton

• Colchester

• Bantry

Swansea •

• Gloucester

• Oxford

LONDON

■ **Cardiff**

• Bristol

• Reading

Thames

• Canterbury

ATLANTIC OCEAN

Exmoor

• Salisbury

• Dover

• Southampton

• Portsmouth

• Brighton

• Folkestone

• Bournemouth

• Exeter

Dartmoor

**Land's
End**

• Plymouth

English Channel

• Penzance

0   50   100   150 Kilometres

0   50   100 Miles

**CHANNEL
ISLANDS**

France

France   Monaco

France is a republic that lies at the heart of western Europe. It stretches from the English Channel in the north to the warm Mediterranean Sea in the south. Western borders are formed by the Atlantic Ocean and by the high peaks of the Pyrenees. To the east rise the Alps, the Jura and Vosges mountains. The French countryside includes plains, the rugged highlands of the Massif Central and beautiful river valleys.

The wide range of climates makes it possible to grow a variety of crops, including wheat, maize, peaches, apples and grapes. French vineyards produce many of the world's finest wines. France is also a major industrial power, specializing in building cars, trains and aircraft. French fashions and perfumes are famous around the world. France is a leading member of the European Union, which it helped to found. Monaco, a tiny independent nation in the southeast, keeps very close links with its much larger neighbour.

In Paris a shining modern pyramid stands side-by-side with the Louvre, a 16th-century palace that now houses one of the world's great art collections. France has been a centre of the arts for over a thousand years.

Pine logs are stacked at a mill in the region of Bordeaux. France has large areas of commercially managed forest in the southwest, as well as in the Massif Central and the east.

France is a land of ancient castles, or châteaux, but these soaring towers are fakes, just a few years old. Disney, the American entertainments corporation, designed this fairytale theme park outside Paris. It is visited by children from all over Europe.

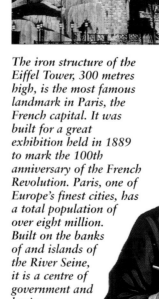

French cooking, or cuisine, is said to be the best in the world, and is much admired. Quiche Lorraine is a pastry tart filled with beaten eggs, cheese, cream, chopped bacon and herbs. Lorraine is in the northeast of the country. Each region of France has its own special dishes.

The iron structure of the Eiffel Tower, 300 metres high, is the most famous landmark in Paris, the French capital. It was built for a great exhibition held in 1889 to mark the 100th anniversary of the French Revolution. Paris, one of Europe's finest cities, has a total population of over eight million. Built on the banks of and islands of the River Seine, it is a centre of government and business.

The Provence region is bordered by Italy, the Mediterranean coast and the Rhône valley. It enjoys mild winters and hot summers. Lavender, grapes, mulberries, olives and citrus fruits grow in its peaceful countryside.

This elderly lacemaker wears the traditional costume of her district in Brittany. The Breton people have their own language, culture and traditions, as do the Catalans and Basques of the southwest and the Corsicans of the Mediterranean. Other citizens are descended from peoples of France's former overseas empire.

N

0   50   100   150   Kilometres
0   50   100 Miles

English Channel

Dunkerque
Calais
Boulogne
Lille
Arras

BELGIUM

LUXEMBOURG

GERMANY

Cherbourg
Dieppe
Amiens
Charleville-Mèzières
Le Havre
Rouen
Reims
Metz
Caen
Seine
Marne
Strasbourg
Nancy
St.-Malo
PARIS
Châlons-sur-Marne
Brest
Chartres
Vosges Mountains
St.-Brieuc
FRANCE
Fontainebleau
Seine
Colmar
Quimper
Rennes
Troyes
Moselle
Mulhouse
Lorient
Le Mans
Orléans
Saône
Rhine
Loire
Dijon
Besançon
Angers
Tours
Doubs
St. Nazaire
Nantes
SWITZERLAND
Cher
Loire
Bourges
Jura Mountains
Poitiers
Saône
Mâcon
La Rochelle
Montluçon
Rhône
Cognac
Limoges
Clermont-Ferrand
Lyon
Isère
Mt. Dore 1886m
St.-Etienne
Mt. Blanc 4807m
Massif Central
Isère
Grenoble
Dordogne
Cère
Valence
Drac
Alps
Bordeaux
Lot
ITALY
Bay of Biscay
Lot
Aveyron
Rhône
Durance
Garonne
Tarn
Avignon
Durance
MONACO
Montauban
Nîmes
Verdon
Biarritz
Toulouse
Montpellier
Aix-en-Provence
Nice
Bayonne
Adour
Garonne
Carcassonne
Béziers
Marseille
Cannes
Pau
Ariège
Aude
Toulon
Lourdes
Pyrenees
Perpignan
Mediterranean Sea
SPAIN
ANDORRA

Bastia
CORSICA (France)
Ajaccio
Bonifacio

Germany

In southern Germany there are evergreen forests and the snowy peaks of the Alps, while in the north there are rolling hills, heath lands and coastal sand dunes. The river Rhine winds through sunny vineyards in the west. Around the rivers Oder and Neisse, along the eastern border, stretch the plains of central Europe. Here the climate is warm in summer but very cold in winter.

In the Middle Ages, Germany was divided into hundreds of small states and cities. The country was united in 1871, but was divided again (into two parts, the Federal Republic of Germany in the west and the German Democratic Republic in the east) between 1945 and 1990, after Germany's defeat in World War II.

Germany today is a Federal Republic, with many laws being made at a regional level. The country is divided into 16 states called *Länder*. Each region has its own spoken dialects of German, style of architecture, customs and traditions. Germany has many large cities. The capital, in the northeast of the country, is Berlin.

Germany is a member of the European Union and is an important centre of industry and trade. The country is famous for its automobile, chemical and electronic industries. Factories employ many workers from other parts of Europe, such as Turkey. The eastern part of Germany which was organized on communist lines before 1990, is going through many industrial changes. Germany has an important tourist industry. Its attractions include medieval castles and winter sports.

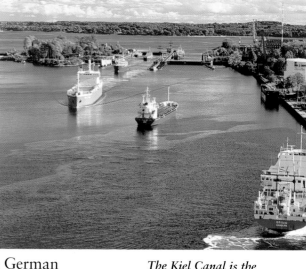

The Kiel Canal is the busiest shipping canal in the world, being used by over 40,000 ships a year. 98 km long, it provides a vital link between the North Sea and the Baltic Sea. Germany's northern coast includes major European ports such as Bremen, Hamburg, Lübeck and Rostock.

Wurst *means sausage and Germany is said to have over 1,500 different kinds, each region having its speciality. Cold meats such as ham are popular for the evening meal, called Abendessen. Other German delicacies are rye breads, tarts and gâteaux, beers and wines.*

Modern office blocks tower above traditional buildings in the city of Frankfurt-am-Main. Frankfurt is the home of the German stock exchange and is a centre of banking and insurance. Many international trade fairs are held in the city.

A tractor harvests sugar beet on the north German plain. Many farms in the south are small and family owned. Farms in the east have always been much larger.

Germany

DENMARK

Baltic Sea

North Sea

Flensburg

Kiel

Stralsund

Neumünster

Rostock

Lübeck

Schwerin

Wilhelmshaven

Bremerhaven

Hamburg

Bremen

Lüneburg

Elbe

Weser

NETHERLANDS

Celle

Aller

BERLIN

Oder

Hannover

Brunswick

Brandenburg

Frankfurt an der Oder

POLAND

Ems

Bielefeld

Weser

Leine

Hildesheim

Magdeburg

Elster

Cottbus

Münster

Harz Mts.

Dessau

Neisse

Rhine

Paderborn

Essen

Dortmund

Halle

Leipzig

Duisburg

Kassel

Elbe

Düsseldorf

Wuppertal

Mühlhausen

Dresden

Cologne

Marburg

Erfurt

Chemnitz

Aachen

Bonn

Gera

Ore Mountains

BELGIUM

Geissen

Zwickau

GERMANY

Plauen

Koblenz

Eifel

Wiesbaden

Main

CZECH REPUBLIC

LUXEMBOURG

Mosel

Rhine

Frankfurt-am-Main

Bayreuth

Mainz

Darmstadt

Bamberg

Trier

Würzburg

Bohemian Forest

Mannheim

Nuremberg

Heidelberg

Regensburg

FRANCE

Karlsruhe

Heilbronn

Danube

Ingolstadt

Passau

Stuttgart

N

Swabian Jura

Augsburg

Rhine

Ulm

Black Forest

Munich

Freiburg

Lake Constance

Alps

AUSTRIA

SWITZERLAND

▲ Zugspitze 2963m

0   50   100 Kilometres
0   25   50   75 Miles

Switzerland and its neighbours

Switzerland is famous for its dairy herds, which produce cheeses such as Emmenthaler and Gruyère. These may be melted in a pot, mixed with white wine, and seasoned to make a fondue. Pieces of bread are dipped into the delicious mixture on special forks.

The Matterhorn rises to 4,478 metres above sea level. This dramatic peak is in the Swiss canton of Valais, near the Italian border. It was in the Alps that mountain climbing first became popular, and many climbers come here each year.

The snowy mountain ranges of the Alps form a massive barrier between northern and southern Europe. Some of the highest peaks are in Germany, France and Italy, but many lie within the borders of three Alpine nations – Switzerland, Liechtenstein and Austria. The ice and rock of the summits give way to green Alpine pastures, filled with wildflowers in summer. These drop steeply towards forested valleys and deep lakes. Melting snows from the Alps are the source of Western Europe's greatest rivers, including the Rhine, the Rhône, the Po and the Inn-Danube river system.

Communications and transport through the Alps have always been very hazardous. Routes to the south now pass through deep tunnels bored through the rock. The Simplon, between Switzerland and Italy, is the world's longest rail tunnel, opened in 1922. It is 19.8 kilometres long. The St Gotthard Road tunnel of 1980, at 16.4 kilometres, holds the world record for any motor vehicle tunnel.

Switzerland is a small country divided into districts called cantons. Four languages may be heard, namely French, German, Italian and Romansh. Although Switzerland has few natural resources apart from hydroelectric power, it has become a wealthy country through the manufacture of clocks, watches and precision instruments. It is a centre of banking and tourism. The spectacular mountain scenery, with its lakes, waterfalls and pretty villages, attracts winter sportsmen and summer holiday makers. Switzerland is neutral, having kept out of European wars since 1815. The city of Geneva is the headquarters of many bodies such as the International Red Cross and the World Health Organization.

To the east, Liechtenstein is a tiny German-speaking state which has managed to avoid being swallowed up by its more powerful neighbours. It is ruled by a prince, but laws are passed by an elected government. It is closely linked with Switzerland and uses the Swiss franc as its currency.

Balzers lies on slopes rising from the valley of the River Rhine, in the extreme south of Liechtenstein. Tourists visit this little Alpine principality in search of mountain scenery and snow for winter skiing.

Switzerland has many colourful festivals. In spring and autumn, herds of goats or cows decorated with flowers and bells are led to and from their summer pastures, high in the mountains. In winter, too, people celebrate saints' days and carnivals.

The white-tailed eagle is a powerful, dark-brown bird of prey with a white, wedge-shaped tail. It is a rare sight soaring over Austrian lakes in winter months. Its main breeding grounds lie to the east, in the Balkans and eastern Europe. Like many European birds of prey, it has suffered from being over-hunted.

Austria

A small country today, Austria once ruled a vast Central European empire. The country is a German-speaking republic, and its capital, Vienna, has many grand historical buildings.

Much of the country is made up of forested mountain slopes, whose timber is used for paper-making, for building the broad-roofed chalets of the Alps and for woodcarving. Many tourists visit the ski-slopes in winter. The east of the country descends to flat lands around the river Danube and this is where most industry and agriculture is based. Austria has few natural resources, but exports textiles, chemicals, electrical goods and machinery. It is a member of the European Union and its major trading partner is Germany.

Switzerland

Liechtenstein

Austria

N

0   50   100   150   200 Kilometres

0   50   100   150 Miles

CZECH REPUBLIC

FRANCE

LIECHTENSTEIN

GERMANY

Basel

Zurich

Linz

Danube

Salzburg

VIENNA

AUSTRIA

■ **BERN**

S w i s s A l p s

Innsbruck

▲ *Grossglockner*
3797m

Graz

Geneva

C e n t r a l A l p s

SWITZERLAND

▲ *Dufourspitze*
4634m

ITALY

HUNGARY

SLOVENIA

Vienna's Burgtheater was built in the 1800s. As capital of the old Austro-Hungarian empire, Vienna was a centre of architecture, opera, popular drama, music, dance and the visual arts. One of the most famous Viennese composers was Johann Strauss the Younger (1835-99), whose popular waltz tunes, such as 'The Blue Danube', became a lasting symbol of the city.

Cut glass is produced at Rattenberg, in the Lower Inn valley of the Tirol. The Alpine lands have enjoyed a long tradition in hand crafts such as wood carving, toy-making, leather work, weaving, felt-making and the delicate decoration of fine porcelain.

Spain and Portugal

Beyond the high mountain ranges of the Pyrenees, the Iberian peninsula juts out from southern Europe between the Atlantic Ocean and the Mediterranean Sea. The land is mostly mountainous, with a broad central plateau. The northwest is green, kept moist by Atlantic rains, but much of the country bakes under the summer sun. It is hot and dusty, and parts are in danger of becoming desert. The region includes many beautiful cities, with palaces and cathedrals dating from the early Middle Ages, when Muslims from North Africa ruled the region, and Christian knights fought against them. The Iberian peninsula produces cork, olives, maize, sunflowers, oranges and grapes for wine, sherry and port. Cattle are bred in many areas and bullfighting is an ancient tradition. Large fishing fleets are based around the coast and the blue seas and sunny beaches attract many tourists. Engineering, chemical and textile production and food processing are major industries.

Paella is a Spanish dish made of rice mixed with seafood, chicken and vegetables, flavoured with garlic and saffron. It is cooked in a big pan and is popular on family occasions.

There are three Iberian nations. The smallest is Andorra, a tiny principality high in the Pyrenees. Portugal is a large republic on the Atlantic coast. The largest is the kingdom of Spain, which stretches all the way from the Bay of Biscay to the Balearic Islands. Both Spain and Portugal are European Union members. Iberian peoples include the Portuguese, Spanish, Galicians, Catalans and the Basques, who speak a language unrelated to any other in Europe.

The Algarve is an area of southern Portugal that has a beautiful coastline. It is very popular with tourists and is a centre for fishing.

The Torre de Belem was built in Lisbon harbour in 1520 to protect ships sailing to and from Lisbon, the Portuguese capital. At this time Portugal was starting to build up a large overseas empire.

Spain is one of the world's largest exporters of citrus fruits. These include sweet mandarins, lemons and oranges from Seville.

Spain

Portugal

Andorra

Bay of Biscay

Santander

San Sebastián

Bilbao

Vitoria

Pamplona

FRANCE

Pyrenees

ANDORRA

Andorra la Vella

Figueras

Gerona

n Mountains

Ebro

Arga

Burgos

Logroño

Gállego

Cinca

Llobregat

Manresa

Tarrasa

Barcelona

Soria

Ebro

Lérida

lladolid

Duero

Saragossa

Reus

Jalón

Caspe

Tarragona

SPAIN

Tortosa

Avila

Tajuna

Tajo

Morella

Guadalajara

Vinaroz

Alcalá de Henares

Teruel

N

MADRID

Mijares

MENORCA

Mahón

MALLORCA

Toledo

Cuenca

Castellón de la Plana

Aranjuez

Turia

Palma

Manacor

Valencia

Guadiana

Villarrobledo

Júcar

IBIZA

Ciudad Real

Albacete

Ibiza

Puertollano

Alcoy

Mediterranean Sea

Segura

Alicante

Linares

Murcia

Córdoba

Lorca

Cartagena

Jaén

Aguilas

Genil

Granada

Sierra Nevada

da

Almería

Every town in Spain has its own fairs, or fiestas. Many of these mark religious festivals, while others commemorate historical events. At Toledo, near Madrid, parades may include figures wearing the masks of giants, devils, clowns and animals.

Málaga

Motril

Marbella

RALTAR (U.K.)

| 0 | 50 | 100 | 150 | Kilometres |
| 0 | 25 | 50 | 75 | Miles |

Italy and its neighbours

Italy is a long, boot-shaped peninsula, stretching southwards into the Mediterranean Sea. The country also includes two large islands, Sicily and Sardinia. The northern mainland takes in the lakes and towering mountains of the Alps and the fertile plains around the river Po. The Apennine Mountains form a rugged backbone down the centre of the country and in the south there are active volcanoes.

The climate of Italy is warm enough for farmers to grow olives, citrus fruits and grapes. Fishing fleets catch tuna and sardines. Many people work in tourism; others work in factories, producing cars, clothes, leather goods and computers. Most industry is based in the wealthier north. Italy was a founding member of the European Union. In ancient times Rome ruled most of western Europe, but Italy was later divided into many small states until it was reunited in 1861. On the peninsula, there are still two tiny independent states. Vatican City is the headquarters of the Roman Catholic Church and San Marino is a republic in the Apennines. Malta is another independent country, with its own language and way of life. These tiny islands lie between Sicily and North Africa. Malta's economy depends on its naval dockyards and on tourism.

Spaghetti served with a Bolognese sauce of meat and tomato is just one of the many pasta dishes that have made Italian cooking popular around the world.

Venice is a fine city built on mud islands on the northern Adriatic coast. It is famous for its canals, bridges and gondolas, which are traditional black boats guided by poles.

St Peter's Square lies within Vatican City, the area of Rome that comes under the rule of the Roman Catholic Church. Many Christians come here to be blessed by the Pope, or to visit the great basilica of St Peter's. The Vatican City or 'Holy See' is the world's smallest independent country. Only 0.44 sq km in area, its population is about 10,000.

Vineyards cover the sunny hillsides of Chianti, in the central region of Tuscany. The grapes produce a strong red wine. Grapes have been grown in Italy for thousands of years. Today it is the biggest wine producer in the world.

Many tourists come to see the Leaning Tower, in the ancient university town of Pisa. Work on the beautiful marble tower began over 800 years ago, but it was built on sinking ground and soon began to tilt over at an angle. It leans over by 5 metres from the vertical.

In Sardinian and Spanish costumes, horsemen take to the streets in Oristano on the island of Sardinia during the Sartiglia Festival, which has celebrated the start of spring since medieval times. The Sards speak their own dialect of Italian and have kept up many ancient traditions. Over the centuries, many different civilizations have invaded Sardinia, each bringing its customs.

0   50   100   150 Kilometres
0   25   50   75   100 Miles

SWITZERLAND

AUSTRIA

A l p s

Bolzano
▲ Mt. Ortles
3905m

Udine

SLOVENIA

Trieste

▲ Mt. Blanc
4807m

Bergamo

Plave

F R A N C E

Milan

Brescia

Verona

Padua

Venice

Turin

Ticino

Oglio

Po

Tanaro

C R O A T I A

▲ Mt. Viso
3841m

Parma

Reno

Modena

Ferrara

Genoa

Bologna

Ravenna

MONACO

La Spezia

Rimini

San Marino

SAN MARINO

A p e n n i n e s

Florence

Pisa

Arno

Ancona

Livorno

Ligurian Sea

Adriatic Sea

Perugia

Bastia

Elba

Terni

Tiber

Pescara

**CORSICA
(France)**

Ajaccio

**VATICAN
CITY**

■ **ROME**

ITALY

Foggia

Bonifacio

Ofanto

Bari

Sassari

Naples

Potenza

Brindisi

Tirso

▲ Mt. Vesuvius
1277m

Salerno

Taranto

Oristano

Senise

**SARDINIA
(Italy)**

Cagliari

Tyrrhenian Sea

Cosenza

Catanzaro

*Revellers wear masks and cloaks
for the carnival in Venice. For
hundreds of years, Venice was
the most important centre for
trade between Europe and the
East, and so became very rich.*

**Lipari
Islands**

Trapani

Palermo

Messina

Reggio di Calabria

**SICILY
(Italy)**

▲ Mt. Etna
3340m

Agrigento

Catania

Syracuse

Mediterranean Sea

N

MALTA

■ **Valletta**

Italy

San Marino

Vatican City

Malta

Central Europe

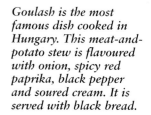

Central Europe

Warsaw, the Polish capital since 1550, lies on the River Vistula. Much of it was rebuilt after bitter fighting during the Second World War (1939-45). Today, Warsaw has a population of over 1,655,000 and is a centre of business, industry, such as car manufacture and communications.

A great plain covers the northern part of Poland. Sunny in the summer, but bitterly cold and snowy in winter, it is drained by the rivers Bug and Vistula. To the south, the land rises to the Tatra Mountains. Polish farmers grow potatoes, flax, rye and beet. Poland has large forests and reserves of coal, sulphur, silver and mineral salt. In some areas the land has been badly polluted by industry.

In 1993 Czechoslovakia, to the south, split into two separate countries, the Czech Republic and the Slovak Republic. These regions include high mountains and forests, wooded hills and fertile farmland. The Czechs produce paper, glass, steel and the original Pilsener beer. The Slovaks mine iron ore, raise pigs and grow cereal crops.

Across the winding River Danube are the plains and rolling hills of Hungary, where vineyards produce strong red wines and orchards supply fruit for preserving and jam-making.

Central Europe is home to Slavic peoples such as the Poles, Czechs and Slovaks, to the Magyar people of Hungary and to Roma (Gypsies), Germans and Jews. In the Middle Ages there were powerful kingdoms in Central Europe, and many beautiful cities date from then. The region later came under the rule of more powerful neighbours such as Turkey, Austria, Russia or Germany. From 1947 until 1990 the whole of Central Europe was ruled by communist governments.

Goulash is the most famous dish cooked in Hungary. This meat-and-potato stew is flavoured with onion, spicy red paprika, black pepper and soured cream. It is served with black bread.

Hungary's Houses of Parliament stand on the River Danube in the capital, Budapest. There are 88 statues outside the building.

Prague, capital and largest city of the Czech Republic, rises from the banks of the River Vltava (below). In the Middle Ages it was capital of a kingdom called Bohemia and was a centre of learning and the arts. Prague, although now industrialized, is still a beautiful old city which has recently become one of the most popular destinations for tourists in Europe.

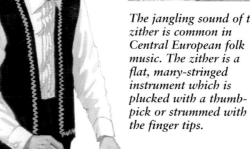

The jangling sound of the zither is common in Central European folk music. The zither is a flat, many-stringed instrument which is plucked with a thumb-pick or strummed with the finger tips.

Slovaks, a Slavic people, make up the majority of the population of Slovakia. This Orthodox church is a fine example of Slavic folk architecture. It is built in a traditional design, with stepped roofs and onion domes.

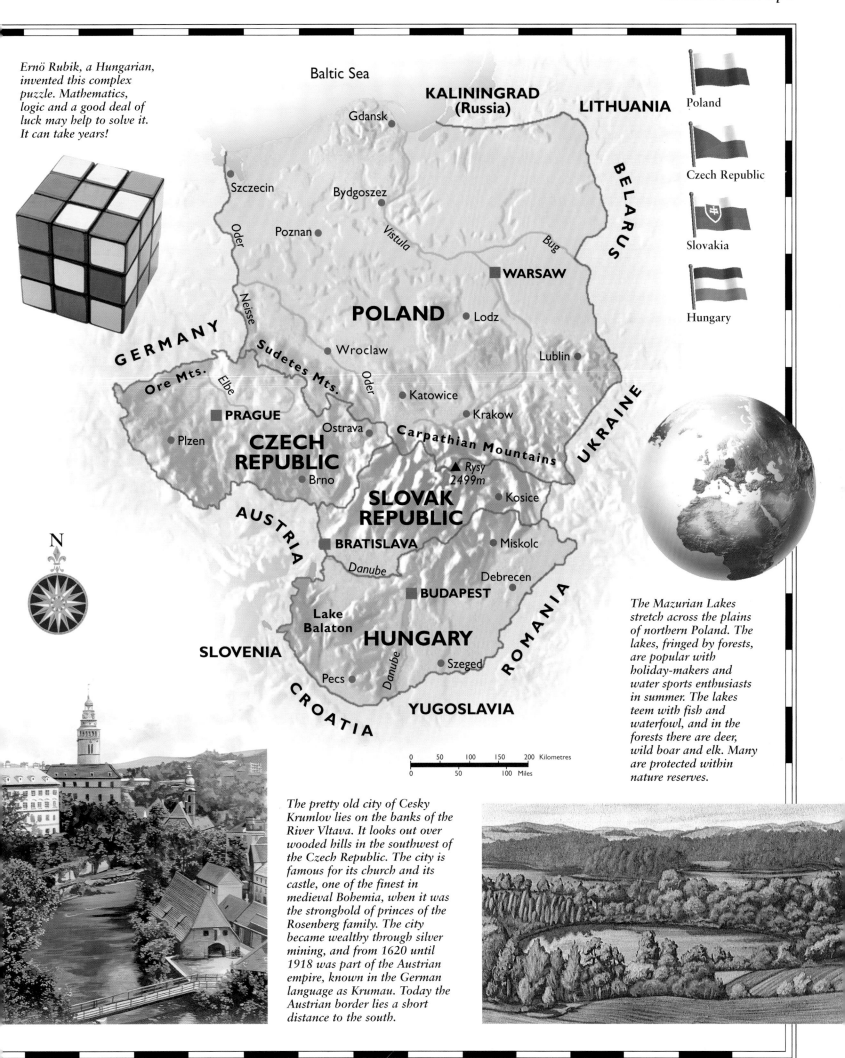

Ernö Rubik, a Hungarian, invented this complex puzzle. Mathematics, logic and a good deal of luck may help to solve it. It can take years!

Baltic Sea

KALININGRAD (Russia)

LITHUANIA

Poland

Czech Republic

Slovakia

Hungary

Gdansk

Szczecin

Bydgoszez

Poznan

Oder

Vistula

Bug

BELARUS

WARSAW

POLAND

Lodz

Neisse

GERMANY

Wroclaw

Sudetes Mts.

Oder

Lublin

Ore Mts.

Elbe

Katowice

UKRAINE

PRAGUE

Krakow

Ostrava

Carpathian Mountains

Plzen

CZECH REPUBLIC

Brno

▲ Rysy 2499m

Kosice

SLOVAK REPUBLIC

AUSTRIA

BRATISLAVA

Miskolc

Danube

Debrecen

N

BUDAPEST

Lake Balaton

ROMANIA

HUNGARY

SLOVENIA

Szeged

Pecs

Danube

CROATIA

YUGOSLAVIA

0   50   100   150   200 Kilometres

0   50   100 Miles

The Mazurian Lakes stretch across the plains of northern Poland. The lakes, fringed by forests, are popular with holiday-makers and water sports enthusiasts in summer. The lakes teem with fish and waterfowl, and in the forests there are deer, wild boar and elk. Many are protected within nature reserves.

The pretty old city of Cesky Krumlov lies on the banks of the River Vltava. It looks out over wooded hills in the southwest of the Czech Republic. The city is famous for its church and its castle, one of the finest in medieval Bohemia, when it was the stronghold of princes of the Rosenberg family. The city became wealthy through silver mining, and from 1620 until 1918 was part of the Austrian empire, known in the German language as Krumau. Today the Austrian border lies a short distance to the south.

The Balkan states

The Balkan peninsula is a broad mass of land that extends southwards from central Europe into the eastern Mediterranean. Its coastline borders the Adriatic, Black Sea and the Mediterranean. Much of the region is rugged and mountainous, with areas of fertile plains. Winters can be bitterly cold in the north and summers can be very hot and dry, especially in the south.

The region is home to many peoples. There are Slavic peoples, such as Slovaks, Slovenians, Croats, Serbs and Bosnian Muslims, as well as Roma (Gypsies), Magyars (Hungarians), Romanians, Bulgars, Turks, Albanians and Greeks. Between 1990 and 1991 the former republic of Yugoslavia broke up into five different nations – Slovenia, Croatia, Bosnia-Herzegovina, Yugoslavia (Serbia-Montenegro) and the Former Yugoslav Republic of Macedonia. Disputes over the new borders led to terrible wars in the early 1990s. Albania and Romania have also suffered unrest in recent years.

The Balkan peninsula becomes narrower to the south of Bulgaria, and breaks up into ragged headlands and island chains. Here is Greece, a land of brown rocks, blue seas, whitewashed villages, ancient ruins and medieval churches. Cities such as Athens are full of wonderful reminders of the ancient Greek civilizations which greatly influenced the European way of life.

Farmers in the Balkans produce maize, sunflowers, melons, grapes for wine, fruit, olives and tobacco. Greece has been a member of the European Union since 1981 and every year attracts tourists from all over the world.

In 1989 there was an uprising in Romania, which had a form of communist government. There were strikes, riots and fighting in the capital, Bucharest. The unpopular ruler, President Nicolae Ceausescu, was overthrown and shot.

The Dalmatian pelican can be seen in the Danube delta. The river Danube forms the border between Romania and Bulgaria before flowing into the Black Sea. Draining the delta wetlands has reduced the number of pelicans in recent years.

The Corinth Canal, over six kilometres long, was opened in 1893. It offers a direct route for shipping travelling from the Gulf of Corinth to Piraeus, the port of Athens. This narrow strip of water separates the large peninsula of the Peloponnesus from the central mainland.

This amphitheatre at Pula in Croatia was built by the Romans in AD80. The whole of the Balkan peninsula was once part of the Roman Empire.

Greek food is popular in many parts of the world. This salad is made from tomatoes, cucumber, black olives and cubes of feta, a white goat's cheese. The dressing of olive oil is mopped up with crusty white bread.

The first Olympic Games were held in Olympia in 776BC. This statue of a discus thrower was made by the Greek sculptor Myron around 450BC.

N

0 100 200 300 Kilometres
0 50 100 150 200 Miles

UKRAINE
MOLDOVA
AUSTRIA
SLOVENIA
Ljubljana
HUNGARY
Zagreb
CROATIA
ROMANIA
Carpathians
BOSNIA-HERZEGOVINA
Transylvanian Alps
Belgrade
Bucharest
Sarajevo
Danube
YUGOSLAVIA
BULGARIA
Black Sea
Adriatic Sea
Sofia
Skopje
MACEDONIA
Tirane
TURKEY
ALBANIA
GREECE
Thessaloníki
Aegean Sea
Pindus Mts.
Athens
Peloponnesus
Kalamai
Rhodes
Khania
Iráklion
Crete

Albania

Romania

Bulgaria

Slovenia

Croatia

Greece

Macedonia

Yugoslavia

Bosnia-Herzegovina

Apples are sorted and packed into crates at this factory in Peshkepi, in eastern Albania. Albanian crops include grapes, wheat, maize, potatoes and beet, but this small, mountainous country has little fertile farmland and the summers are hot and dusty.

The Iron Gates are part of the spectacular gorge of Samaria on the island of Crete. This large Mediterranean island is a part of Greece. Many tourists visit its beautiful mountains and coastline and its ancient ruins, some of which date back over 4,000 years.

The medieval Church of St John at Caneo, by Lake Ohrid in the Former Yugoslav Republic of Macedonia. Greece has disputed the right of this new country to use the name Macedonia, the same name as the ancient Greek kingdom in the north of Greece.

Russia and its neighbours

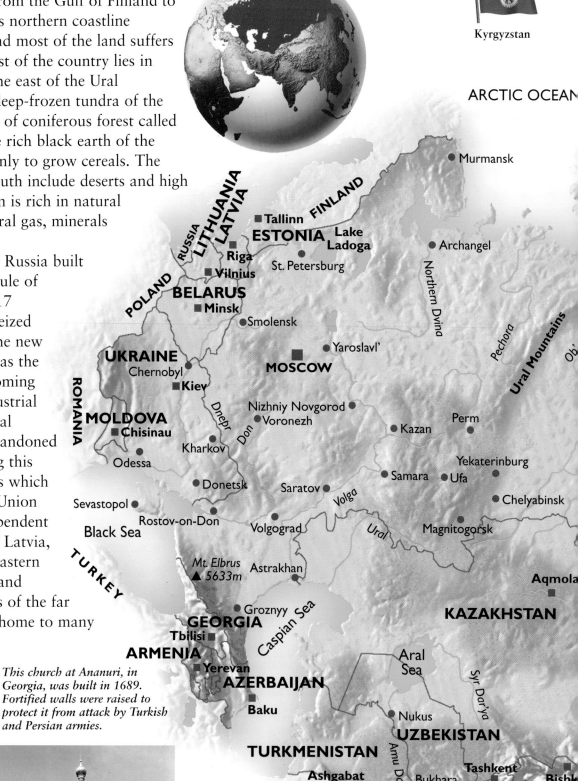

The Russian Federation is the world's biggest country, stretching from the Gulf of Finland to the Pacific Ocean. Its northern coastline borders the Arctic Ocean, and most of the land suffers from severe winters. The west of the country lies in Europe, while the lands to the east of the Ural Mountains lie in Asia. The deep-frozen tundra of the far north gives way to a belt of coniferous forest called taiga. In the southwest is the rich black earth of the steppes, grasslands used mainly to grow cereals. The neighbouring lands to the south include deserts and high mountains. The whole region is rich in natural resources including oil, natural gas, minerals and timber.

From the 1500s onwards Russia built up a vast empire under the rule of emperors called tsars. In 1917 communist revolutionaries seized power and killed the tsar. The new state, which became known as the Soviet Union, set about becoming one of the world's great industrial powers. It underwent political reforms in the 1980s and abandoned communism in 1990. During this period many of the countries which had been part of the Soviet Union broke away to become independent nations – the Baltic states of Latvia, Lithuania and Estonia, the eastern European states of Ukraine and Belarus, and the borderlands of the far south. Russia itself remains home to many different ethnic groups.

Armenia

Kyrgyzstan

ARCTIC OCEAN

Murmansk

LITHUANIA
LATVIA
RUSSIA
FINLAND
Tallinn
ESTONIA
Lake Ladoga
Archangel
Riga
St. Petersburg
Vilnius
POLAND
BELARUS
Minsk
Smolensk
Northern Dvina
Pechora
Ural Mountains
Ob'
UKRAINE
Chernobyl
Yaroslavl'
MOSCOW
Kiev
ROMANIA
Dnepr
Nizhniy Novgorod
Voronezh
Kazan
Perm
MOLDOVA
Chisinau
Don
Yekaterinburg
Kharkov
Samara
Ufa
Odessa
Saratov
Chelyabinsk
Donetsk
Volga
Sevastopol
Rostov-on-Don
Volgograd
Ural
Magnitogorsk
Black Sea
TURKEY
Mt. Elbrus
▲ 5633m
Astrakhan
Aqmola
Groznyy
Caspian Sea
KAZAKHSTAN
GEORGIA
Tbilisi
ARMENIA
Aral Sea
Yerevan
AZERBAIJAN
Syr Dar'ya
Baku
Nukus
UZBEKISTAN
TURKMENISTAN
Amu Dar'ya
Ashgabat
Bukhara
Tashkent
Bishk
IRAN
Dushanbe
TAJIKISTAN
AFGHANISTAN

St Basil's Cathedral is in Moscow's Red Square. Many Russian Orthodox churches have beautiful, onion-shaped domes.

This church at Ananuri, in Georgia, was built in 1689. Fortified walls were raised to protect it from attack by Turkish and Persian armies.

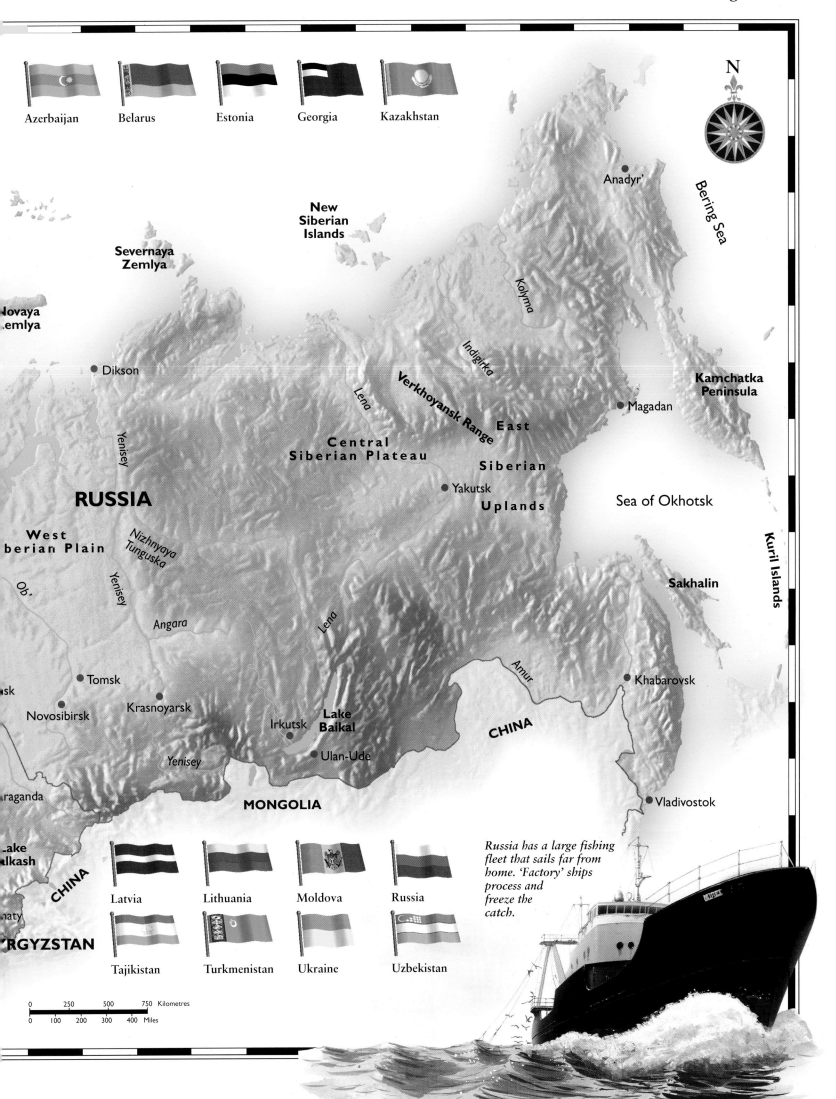

Azerbaijan

Belarus

Estonia

Georgia

Kazakhstan

N

Anadyr'

Bering Sea

New
Siberian
Islands

Severnaya
Zemlya

Novaya
Zemlya

Kolyma

Indigirka

Dikson

Kamchatka
Peninsula

Verkhoyansk Range

Lena

East

Magadan

Yenisey

Central
Siberian Plateau

Siberian

Yakutsk

RUSSIA

Uplands

Sea of Okhotsk

West
Siberian Plain

Nizhnyaya
Tunguska

Ob'

Yenisey

Sakhalin

Kuril Islands

Angara

Lena

Tomsk

Amur

Khabarovsk

Krasnoyarsk

Novosibirsk

Irkutsk

Lake
Baikal

CHINA

Yenisey

Ulan-Ude

Karaganda

MONGOLIA

Vladivostok

Lake
Balkash

CHINA

*Russia has a large fishing
fleet that sails far from
home. 'Factory' ships
process and
freeze the
catch.*

Latvia

Lithuania

Moldova

Russia

Almaty

KYRGYZSTAN

Tajikistan

Turkmenistan

Ukraine

Uzbekistan

| 0 | 250 | 500 | 750 | Kilometres |
| 0 | 100 | 200 | 300 | 400 | Miles |

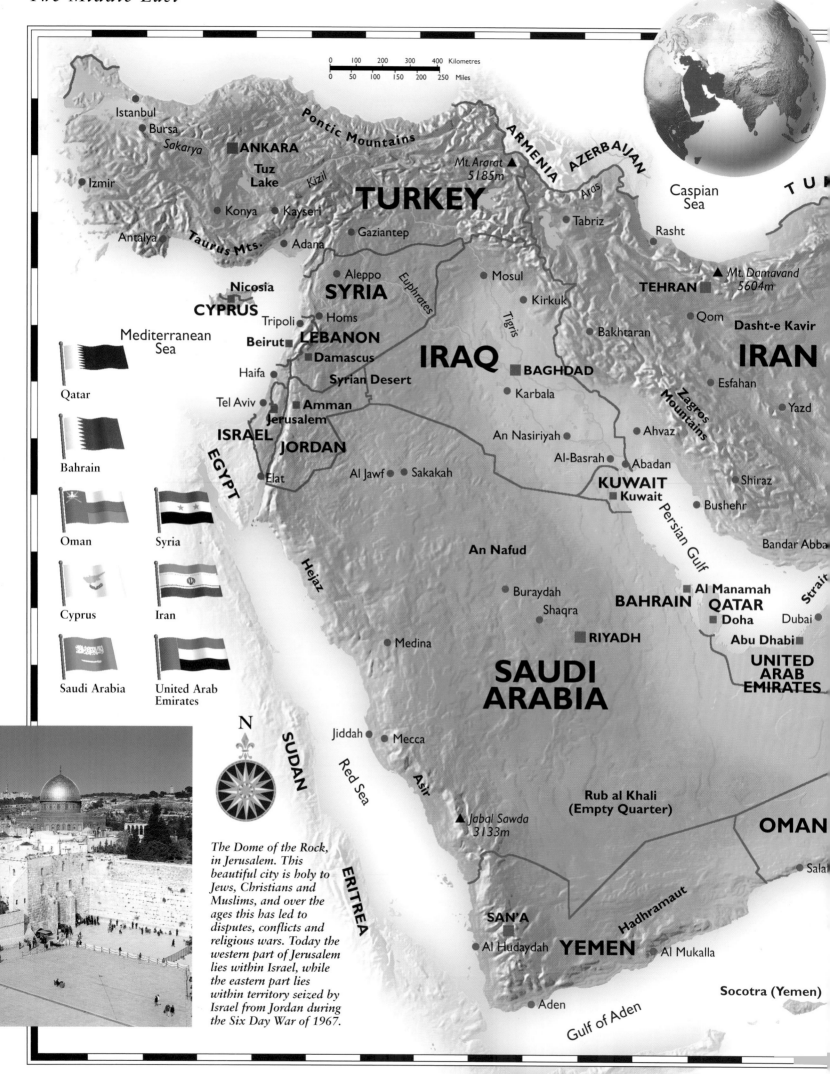

0 100 200 300 400 Kilometres
0 50 100 150 200 250 Miles

Istanbul
Bursa
Sakarya
Izmir
ANKARA
Konya
Kayseri
Antalya
Taurus Mts.
Adana
Gaziantep
TURKEY
Pontic Mountains
Mt. Ararat
5185m
ARMENIA
Aras
AZERBAIJAN
Caspian
Sea
Tabriz
Rasht
TEHRAN
Mt. Damavand
5604m
Qom
*Tuz
Lake*
Kizil

Nicosia
CYPRUS
Aleppo
SYRIA
Tripoli
Homs
Euphrates
Mosul
Kirkuk
Tigris
Bakhtaran
IRAN
Dasht-e Kavir
Esfahan
Yazd

Mediterranean
Sea
Beirut
LEBANON
Damascus
Haifa
Syrian Desert
IRAQ
BAGHDAD
Karbala
*Zagros
Mountains*
Ahvaz

Tel Aviv
Amman
Jerusalem
ISRAEL
JORDAN
EGYPT
Elat
Al Jawf
Sakakah
An Nasiriyah
Al-Basrah
Abadan
KUWAIT
Kuwait
Shiraz
Bushehr
Persian Gulf
Bandar Abba
Strait

Hejaz
An Nafud
Buraydah
Shaqra
BAHRAIN
Al Manamah
QATAR
Doha
Dubai
Abu Dhabi
Medina
RIYADH
**UNITED
ARAB
EMIRATES**

N

SUDAN
Jiddah
Mecca
Red Sea
Asir
**SAUDI
ARABIA**
Jabal Sawda
3133m
**Rub al Khali
(Empty Quarter)**
OMAN

ERITREA
SAN'A
Al Hudaydah
YEMEN
Al Mukalla
Hadhramaut
Aden
Gulf of Aden
Socotra (Yemen)
Sal

Flags:

Qatar

Bahrain

Oman

Syria

Cyprus

Iran

Saudi Arabia

United Arab
Emirates

*The Dome of the Rock,
in Jerusalem. This
beautiful city is holy to
Jews, Christians and
Muslims, and over the
ages this has led to
disputes, conflicts and
religious wars. Today the
western part of Jerusalem
lies within Israel, while
the eastern part lies
within territory seized by
Israel from Jordan during
the Six Day War of 1967.*

The Middle East

Iraq

Turkey

Israel

Jordan

The Middle East is bordered to the north by mountains, by the rolling grasslands or steppes of eastern Europe and by the Caspian and Black Sea coasts. To the west is the Mediterranean Sea and to the south the warm waters of the Red Sea, Persian Gulf and Indian Ocean. There are fertile lands in the north and west and along the rivers Tigris and Euphrates. However, much of the area, including the vast Arabian peninsula, are taken up by harsh, empty desert.

This part of Asia is sometimes called the 'Near East' or Southwest Asia. It was here that humans first began to farm and build towns, over 12,000 years ago. Three of the world's most widespread religions – Judaism, Christianity and Islam grew up here.

The Middle East is populated by Greeks, Jews, Arabs, Turks, Kurds and Iranians. There are many political and religious conflicts in the region, threatening peace in Cyprus, Israel, Turkey, Iraq, Iran and Kuwait. The most important resource is oil, which has brought great wealth to the families who rule the Arab states around the Gulf. Supertankers carry oil from these deserts to ports all over the world.

Petra is a ruined city in Jordan, in which the buildings are carved out of the cliffs. The city once lay on important trading routes and was capital of the Nabatean kingdom until AD 106, when it was conquered by the ancient Romans.

The Madrasa-i Chahar Bagh (right), in the Iranian city of Isfahan, has been a centre of religious study since the 1700s. Iran is a strictly Islamic country where religious leaders have a major say in government.

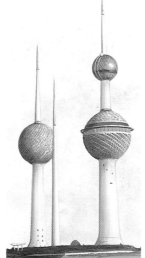

These unusual looking towers are part of a desalination scheme in Kuwait. This useful but expensive process takes the salt out of seawater to make it drinkable. Supplying enough water for drinking and irrigation is a major problem in the desert states around the Gulf.

In the Cappadocia region of Turkey, near Konya, strange rock formations tower above the plains. Homes have been carved out of the rocks and built on to them, making them look like beehives.

Quinces stuffed with minced lamb and flavoured with cinnamon make up an Iranian dish that has been cooked since the days of the ancient Persians. Iranian meals may be served with black tea and large, flat, freshly baked nan breads.

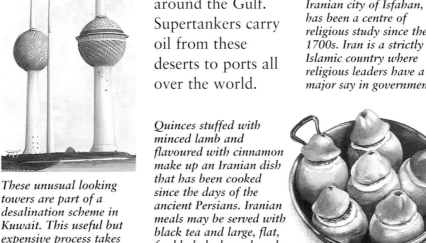

This massive castle in Syria (below) is called Krak des Chevaliers. It dates back to 1205. In the Middle Ages, Christian and Muslim armies fought for control of Palestine or 'Holy Land', in wars called Crusades.

Yemen

Kuwait

Lebanon

Gulf of Oman

MUSCAT

Jabal Ash Sham 3035m

Sur

Mashhad

Zahedan

NISTAN

sht-e Lut

man

sk

India and its neighbours

The Himalaya mountain range, which includes many of the world's highest peaks, separates the great mass of land known as the Indian subcontinent from central Asia and China. Melting snows feed great rivers such as the Ganges which spill across the plains of northern India. The mountainous nations of the north are sparsely populated, while the lands to the south – Pakistan, Bangladesh, India and Myanmar (Burma) – are very crowded. The island nation of Sri Lanka lies in the Indian Ocean, across the Palk Strait.

The subcontinent extends south to the tropics, where it is extremely hot, with winds and torrential rains during the monsoon season.

India and the neighbouring lands make up a melting pot of many different peoples, cultures and languages. These have shaped some of history's greatest civilizations, and the region is the birthplace of many religions, including Hinduism, Buddhism, Sikhism and Jainism. Afghanistan, Pakistan and Bangladesh are Muslim countries, and there are also many Muslims within the borders of India.

The region often suffers from earthquakes, drought and flooding, and poverty is widespread. Crops include wheat, rice, coconuts, sugar-cane, tea and cotton. Factories produce textiles, vehicles, steel, fertilizers and computer software. India has a large film industry based in the city of Bombay.

Kathakali is a form of traditional dancing to be seen in southern India. The dancers, with painted faces and dressed in traditional costumes, retell ancient stories about the Hindu gods and demons.

Elephants and dancers parade through the streets of Kandy, in Sri Lanka, in a great procession, or 'perahera'. It is held each summer to honour a holy relic of the Buddha.

Htamin le thoke is a dish eaten in Myanmar (Burma). It includes all sorts of snacks made from leftovers – noodles, rice, spinach or onions. It is served with tamarind sauce. Tamarind seeds and pulp come from the pod of a tropical tree.

Kashmir is a beautiful region of high valleys, snowy peaks and lakes. It stretches across the Himalaya range on the borders of India, Pakistan and China. Most Kashmiris are Muslims, and some of them have fought a campaign to break away from the Indian state.

The river Ganges forms a maze of waterways before it reaches the Bay of Bengal. Many of the villages on its banks and islands are at risk from flooding during the monsoon rains.

This street market is in Goa, on India's west coast near Hubli-Dharwar. Indian markets are crowded with traders, people haggling over prices, fortune-tellers and showmen. All kinds of food, clothes, tools, pots and pans are on sale. Markets in Goa might specialize in selling coconuts, tropical fruits such as bananas, rice and delicious fresh fish caught locally in the Indian Ocean.

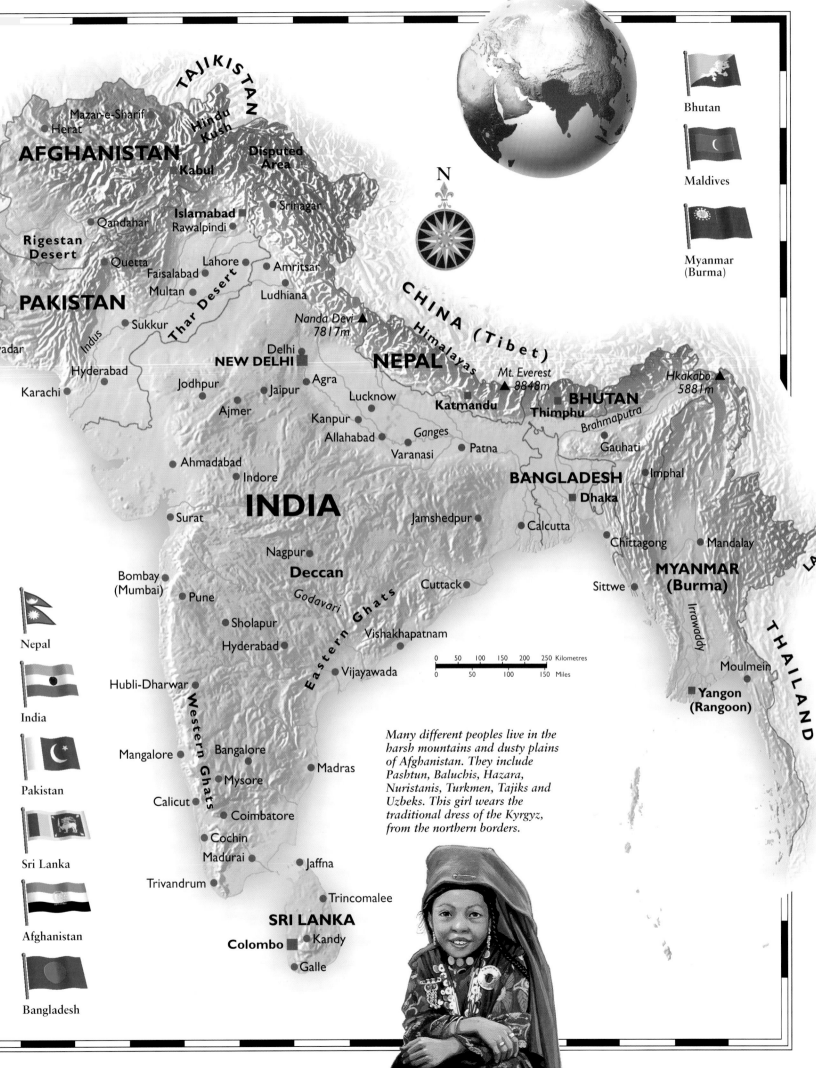

AFGHANISTAN

Herat
Mazar-e-Sharif

TAJIKISTAN

Hindu Kush

Kabul
Qandahar

Disputed Area

Islamabad
Rawalpindi

Srinagar

Rigestan Desert

PAKISTAN

Quetta

Lahore
Faisalabad
Multan

Amritsar

Ludhiana

CHINA (Tibet)

vadar

Indus

Sukkur

Thar Desert

Nanda Devi
7817m

Himalayas

Hyderabad

NEW DELHI

Delhi

NEPAL

Mt. Everest
8848m

Hkakabo
5881m

Karachi

Jodhpur

Agra

Jaipur

Lucknow

Katmandu

BHUTAN
Thimphu

Ajmer

Kanpur

Brahmaputra

Allahabad

Ganges

Gauhati

Ahmadabad

Varanasi

Patna

Indore

BANGLADESH

Imphal

INDIA

Jamshedpur

Dhaka

Surat

Nagpur

Calcutta

Chittagong

Mandalay

Bombay
(Mumbai)

Deccan

Pune

Godavari

Cuttack

MYANMAR
(Burma)

Sholapur

Eastern Ghats

Sittwe

LAOS

Hyderabad

Vishakhapatnam

Irrawaddy

Vijayawada

THAILAND

Hubli-Dharwar

Western Ghats

Moulmein

Mangalore

Bangalore

Madras

Yangon
(Rangoon)

Mysore

Calicut

Coimbatore

Cochin

Madurai

Jaffna

Trivandrum

Trincomalee

SRI LANKA

Colombo

Kandy

Galle

N

Bhutan

Maldives

Myanmar
(Burma)

Nepal

India

Pakistan

Sri Lanka

Afghanistan

Bangladesh

0   50   100   150   200   250 Kilometres
0   50   100   150 Miles

Many different peoples live in the harsh mountains and dusty plains of Afghanistan. They include Pashtun, Baluchis, Hazara, Nuristanis, Turkmen, Tajiks and Uzbeks. This girl wears the traditional dress of the Kyrgyz, from the northern borders.

China and its neighbours

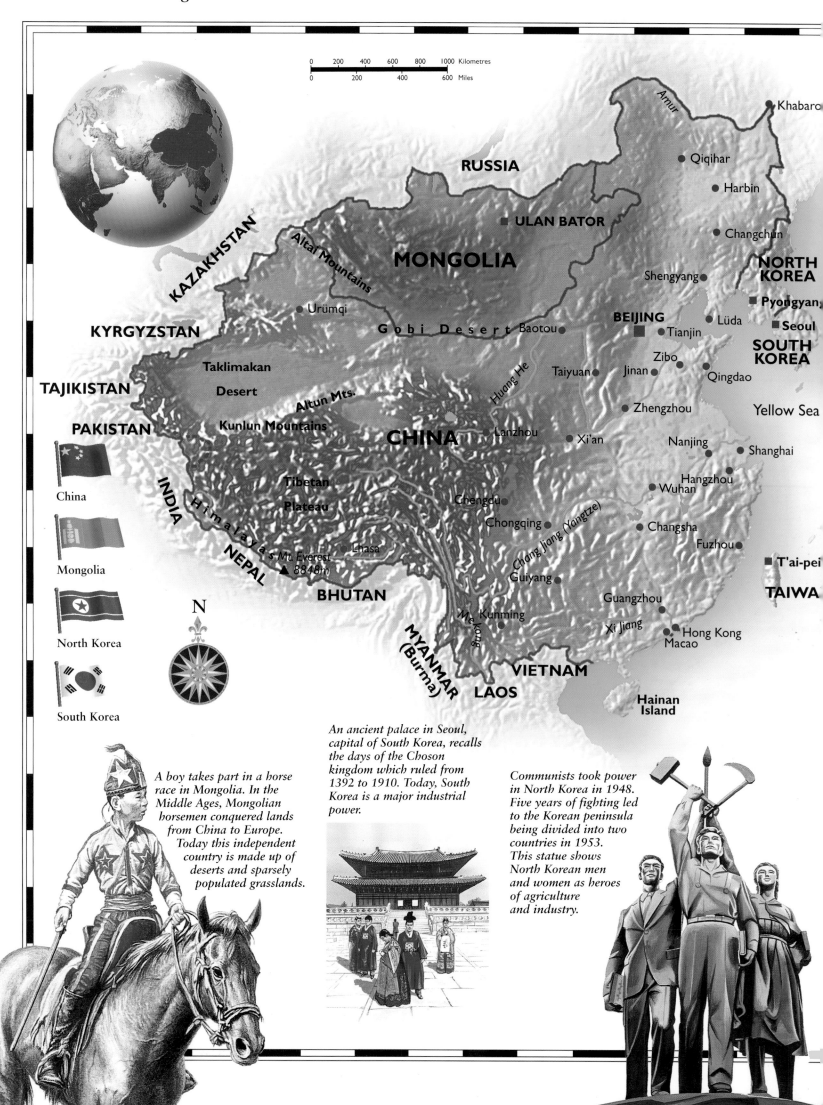

0 200 400 600 800 1000 Kilometres
0 200 400 600 Miles

RUSSIA

Khabaro

Qiqihar

Harbin

ULAN BATOR

Changchun

MONGOLIA

NORTH
KOREA

Shengyang

Pyongyan

Altai Mountains

KAZAKHSTAN

Lüda

BEIJING

Urümqi

Gobi Desert Baotou

Tianjin

Seoul

KYRGYZSTAN

SOUTH
KOREA

Zibo

Taiyuan

Jinan

Qingdao

Taklimakan

Huang He

Zhengzhou

Yellow Sea

TAJIKISTAN

Desert

Altun Mts.

CHINA

Lanzhou

Xi'an

Nanjing

Shanghai

PAKISTAN

Kunlun Mountains

Hangzhou

Wuhan

China

Tibetan

Chengdu

Plateau

INDIA

Changsha

Chongqing

Fuzhou

Chang Jiang (Yangtze)

Himalayas

Lhasa

Mt. Everest
8848m

Guiyang

T'ai-pei

Mongolia

NEPAL

TAIWA

N

BHUTAN

Guangzhou

Mekong

Kunming

North Korea

Xi Jiang

Hong Kong

Macao

MYANMAR
(Burma)

VIETNAM

South Korea

LAOS

Hainan
Island

A boy takes part in a horse
race in Mongolia. In the
Middle Ages, Mongolian
horsemen conquered lands
from China to Europe.
Today this independent
country is made up of
deserts and sparsely
populated grasslands.

An ancient palace in Seoul,
capital of South Korea, recalls
the days of the Choson
kingdom which ruled from
1392 to 1910. Today, South
Korea is a major industrial
power.

Communists took power
in North Korea in 1948.
Five years of fighting led
to the Korean peninsula
being divided into two
countries in 1953.
This statue shows
North Korean men
and women as heroes
of agriculture
and industry.

China and its neighbours

More people live in China than in any other country in the world. This vast country is ringed by remote deserts and towering mountain ranges. Great rivers rise in the mountains and flow across the crowded, fertile plains of the south and east. The coastline borders the Yellow Sea and the East and South China seas. Northern regions have bitterly cold winters, while the south is warm and humid.

Many different peoples live in China, including Tibetans, Uygurs, Mongols and Zhuang. Nine out of ten Chinese belong to the Han ethnic group. China has one of the world's most ancient civilizations and for thousands of years it was ruled by powerful emperors. In 1949 the Chinese Communist Party seized power. It is still in power today, but its economic polices have changed a great deal in recent years. China grows tea, rice, maize and wheat. Industries include textiles, oil, steel, engineering, electronics and household goods.

In 1949 Chinese people who opposed communism set up their own government on the island of Taiwan. The British colony of Hong Kong returned to Chinese rule in 1997. The Portuguese colony of Macao will follow in 1999. China's neighbours include Mongolia, and North and South Korea.

Chow mein is a southern Chinese dish made up of noodles, shredded chicken or meat and stir-fried vegetables. Chinese people who have settled in other lands have made their food popular all around the world.

Tiantan, the Temple of Heaven, is one of the most beautiful sights in Beijing, the Chinese capital. It dates back to 1420. The Chinese emperors used to come here to pray for a good harvest. Many beautiful buildings may still be seen in Beijing, although large areas of the old city have been cleared to make way for new roads.

In the Middle Kingdom theme park in Hong Kong costumed stilt walkers celebrate the Chinese Spring Festival (New Year) in traditional style. Each new year is named after a different animal.

Water buffalo cross the Li Jiang at Yangshuo, near Guilin. In the background are limestone rock formations, a favourite subject for Chinese artists over the ages. Many tourists visit this beautiful region of southern China. While many Chinese cities are huge industrial centres, wide areas of the countryside remain peaceful and unspoiled.

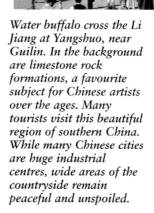

Herbal medicines are sold on the streets of Hong Kong. Chinese doctors use both western medicine and many traditional cures. These may be made up of herbs, roots and leaves as well as parts of animals. The Chinese also treat illnesses with needles, using a method known as acupuncture.

Japan

Japan is a country made up of islands. There are about 3,000 of them in all, forming a long chain down the Pacific coast of northern Asia. The largest and most populated islands are called Hokkaido, Honshu, Shikoku and Kyushu.

Because much of the land is mountainous, most people live on the crowded coastal plains, where there are very big cities. Like many Pacific nations, Japan lies within an earthquake danger zone. Its highest mountain, Fuji, is a volcano. The climate in the north of Japan is cool, with heavy snowfall in winter. The south is mild, however, with warm, humid summers. There is a rainy season in June and July and fierce storms called typhoons may rage across the coasts in September.

Most of the population is Japanese, but there are Korean and Chinese minorities. In the far north are the Ainu, a pale-skinned people who were probably the first inhabitants of the islands. Many Japanese have settled in other parts of the world, such as the United States.

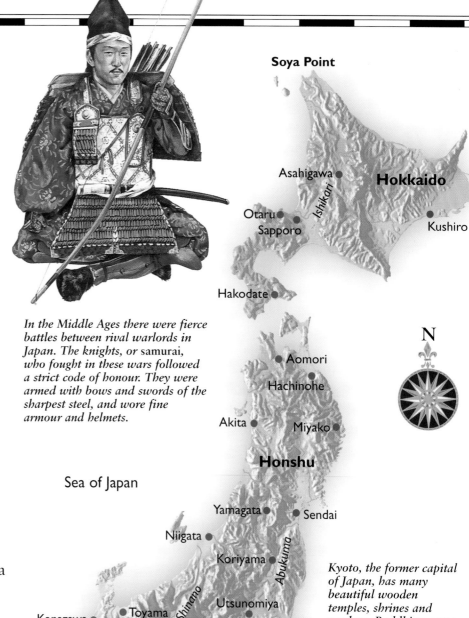

In the Middle Ages there were fierce battles between rival warlords in Japan. The knights, or samurai, who fought in these wars followed a strict code of honour. They were armed with bows and swords of the sharpest steel, and wore fine armour and helmets.

Kyoto, the former capital of Japan, has many beautiful wooden temples, shrines and gardens. Buddhism came to Japan from China in AD552, and many of its beliefs merged with those of the native Shinto religion. Many Japanese respect both Buddhist and Shinto traditions.

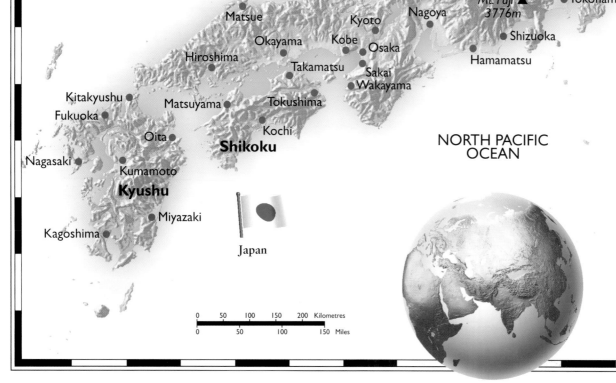

Soya Point

Asahigawa
Otaru
Sapporo
Hokkaido
Kushiro
Ishikari

Hakodate

N

Aomori
Hachinohe
Akita
Miyako

Honshu

Sea of Japan

Yamagata
Sendai
Niigata
Koriyama
Abukuma
Utsunomiya
Mito
Shinano
Kanazawa
Toyama
Takasaki

JAPAN
TOKYO ■
Chiba
Yokohama
Nagoya
Mt. Fuji ▲
3776m
Shizuoka

Matsue
Kyoto
Kobe
Okayama
Osaka
Hiroshima
Takamatsu
Hamamatsu
Sakai
Wakayama

Kitakyushu
Matsuyama
Tokushima
Fukuoka
Kochi
Oita
Shikoku
Nagasaki
Kumamoto
Kyushu

NORTH PACIFIC
OCEAN

Miyazaki
Kagoshima

Japan

| 0 | 50 | 100 | 150 | 200 | Kilometres |
| 0 | 50 | | 100 | 150 | Miles |

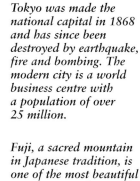

Land of the Rising Sun

In the Japanese language, Japan is called 'Nippon', which means 'Source of the Sun'. The national flag shows a red sunrise. Respect for tradition and the forces of nature survive in the Japanese religion called Shinto.

Japan is said to have been ruled by emperors since 660BC. Its ancient civilization, influenced by that of China, produced the finest pottery, silk textiles, architecture and paintings. The same skills may be seen in modern industrial design.

In the 1930s and 40s Japan attacked and invaded many other Asian countries, before being defeated by the Allies in 1945. Two Japanese cities were destroyed by terrible atomic bombs. Japan recovered rapidly, however. Although it had few natural resources, it became one of the world's greatest economic powers, producing electronic goods and cars. Finance and banking have become major industries.

Japan makes the most of the small amount of good farmland it does have. Its chief crop is rice, and it also grows tea, fruit, soya beans, wheat, barley and sweet potatoes. Japanese fishing fleets find a ready market for their catches back home, where fish forms a big part of their diet.

Tokyo was made the national capital in 1868 and has since been destroyed by earthquake, fire and bombing. The modern city is a world business centre with a population of over 25 million.

Fuji, a sacred mountain in Japanese tradition, is one of the most beautiful mountains in the world. Its volcanic slopes, topped with snow, have been a favourite subject for Japanese artists through the ages.

Sushi is a treat for the eye as well as the tastebuds. Beautifully prepared and displayed snacks of raw fish, vegetables, seaweed and prawns are served with small mounds of rice.

Buyo *means dance in Japanese and traditional Japanese dancers train for many years. The movements are centuries old and are accompanied by a shamisen, a three-stringed instrument.*

Sumo wrestling is a popular sport in Japan. The heavyweight wrestlers aim to make their opponent's body touch the ground. The action is usually over within seconds. However, the wrestlers spend long hours preparing for the contest with special exercises and rituals.

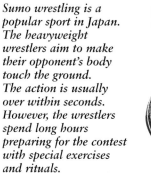

59

Southeast Asia

The part of Asia extending eastwards from India and southwards from China is sometimes called Indo-China. This region takes in Myanmar, Thailand, Laos, Cambodia and Vietnam. Jungle-covered hills slope down to fertile plains crossed by great rivers such as the Irrawaddy and the Mekong. The climate is hot and humid with seasonal heavy, monsoon rains.

A long, thin peninsula stretches southwards to Malaysia and the small city state of Singapore. Malaysia, Indonesia, Brunei and the Philippines occupy the long chains of islands that stretch eastwards into the Pacific Ocean.

The region is home to a great variety of peoples, cultures, religions and languages. Southeast Asia was torn apart by war from the 1940s until the 1970s. The regional economy depends on rice and fruit farming, forestry, rubber and palm oil. Natural resources include oil and natural gas. Tourism, already a major industry in Thailand and Bali, is growing in countries such as Vietnam. Big cities such as Singapore and Jakarta are centres of international business and finance.

Rice has been farmed on these flooded terraces, on the Philippine island of Luzon, for over 2,000 years. In recent years new, improved strains of rice have been developed at research stations in the Philippines.

Bangkok, the capital of Thailand, has hundreds of beautiful Buddhist temples. Buddhism plays a big part in the lives of the Thai people, many of whom become monks who wear orange robes and shave their heads.

The Indonesian island of Bali is famous for its beautiful religious festivals and its court and temple dances. The Balinese follow the Hindu faith, whereas most Indonesians are Muslims.

Vietnamese women wash a crop of carrots in the Mekong River. The vegetables are placed in big wicker baskets. The women protect their heads from the hot sun with the large straw hats that are popular in the lands around the South China Sea.

Buddha Park, outside the Laotian capital of Vientiane, contains many large religious statues. The park was set aside in the 1950s in order to honour both the Buddhist and Hindu faiths.

Satay is a popular dish in Malaysia and other Southeast Asian countries. Small pieces of meat or chicken are placed on a wooden skewer and barbecued, before being served with a hot peanut sauce.

N

Brunei   Laos   Malaysia   Thailand   Vietnam   Indonesia

Cambodia

Philippines

Singapore

CHINA

MYANMAR
(Burma)

Red

Hanoi   ▪ Haiphong

Chiang Mai

LAOS

Vientiane ▪

THAILAND

Mekong

Da Nang

Bangkok ▪

CAMBODIA   VIETNAM

Nha Trang

Phnom Penh ▪

Ho Chi Minh City

Gulf of
Thailand

South China Sea

Luzon   PACIFIC
OCEAN

Manila ▪

PHILIPPINES

Cebu

Sulu Sea

Mindanao

Zamboanga ▪   Davao

Bandar Seri Begawan

BRUNEI

EASTERN
MALAYSIA

B o r n e o

Celebes Sea

Ipoh ●

MALAYSIA

Medan ●

Kuala Lumpur ▪

SINGAPORE

Batanghari

Padang ●

Sumatra

Jambi ●

Palembang ●

Kapuas

Pontianak ●

Balikpapan ●

Barito

Banjarmasin ●

Sulawesi
(Celebes)

Java Sea

Ujung Pandang ●

Jakarta ▪   I N D O N E S I A

Bandung ●   Java   Surabaya

Malang ●   Bali   Flores   Timor

Timor Sea

*These children have
dressed up in fancy
costumes in order to
celebrate Brunei's
Independence Day.
Brunei's population
includes both Malays and
Chinese. This small
nation on the coast of
Borneo gained full
independence from Great
Britain in 1984.*

0   100   200   300   400   500 Kilometres

0   100   200   300 Miles

61

North Africa

The Sahara desert is one of the hottest places on Earth, a shimmering wilderness of sand, rock and gravel which stretches across the continent. The Atlas Mountains run along the desert's northwestern fringes, descending to the fertile Mediterranean coast of the 'Maghreb' lands – Algeria, Morocco and Tunisia. The 'Sahel' lands, those to the south of the Sahara, have sparse, dusty grassland and suffer from droughts, when many people go hungry.

Egypt too is a land of deserts, but the river Nile brings valuable water to its farmland. Thanks to this, Egypt became the centre of an ancient civilization whose splendid temples and tombs may still be seen today. Branches of the Nile also flow through Sudan, Africa's largest country, and through the mountainous lands of Ethiopia.

North Africa is home to the Berbers and to the Arabs, who conquered the region in the AD600s. In the south there are many different Black African peoples, such as the Nuer, Dinka and Shilluk of Sudan, the Amhara of Ethiopia, and the Hausa, Fulani and Kanuri of the Sahel. Most of the region is Muslim, but there are Christians in Egypt, Ethiopia and southern Sudan.

A Berber water-seller offers passers-by a cool drink from his goatskin sack. Many Berbers live in the Atlas Mountains and on the fringes of the Sahara desert. Some are farmers while others are nomadic herders and traders.

A mysterious statue, known as the Sphinx, guards the ancient royal tombs of the pyramids. They stand on the edge of the desert at Giza, near the modern Egyptian capital of Cairo. The ancient Egyptian civilization thrived from about 3100 until 1085BC. Its rulers were called pharaohs.

Beg wot is a thick stew made in Ethiopia. It is cooked with meat, tomatoes and hot peppers. Here, it is served with basil leaves and aubergines on a doughy bread called injera. Ethiopian farmers raise cattle and crops, but food is often scarce.

Goat skins are dyed in big vats in Morocco, particularly in Fez and Marrakesh. The smell from these vats is horrible, because pigeon droppings are used during the dyeing process. The country is famous for its fine crafts, particularly soft leather, woollen rugs, brass and copper. Many of these are bought by tourists in the markets or souks.

PORTUGAL

MADEIRA IS.

Tangier
Rabat
Casablanca
MOROCCO
Marrakesh
Atlas M

CANARY IS.

Ifni

WESTERN SAHARA

MAURITANIA   **MA**

■ **Nouakchott**

Timbuktu

Sénégal   • Kaédi

SENEGAL

Niger

• Kayes

Ségou

GUINEA   ■ **Bamako**

BURKINA FASO

CÔTE D'IVOIRE

A piper plays a traditional instrument at a festival at Ghadamis, in Libya. Arabic music and dialects of the Arabic language are still heard throughout the countries of the North African coast, as they have been since the seventh century.

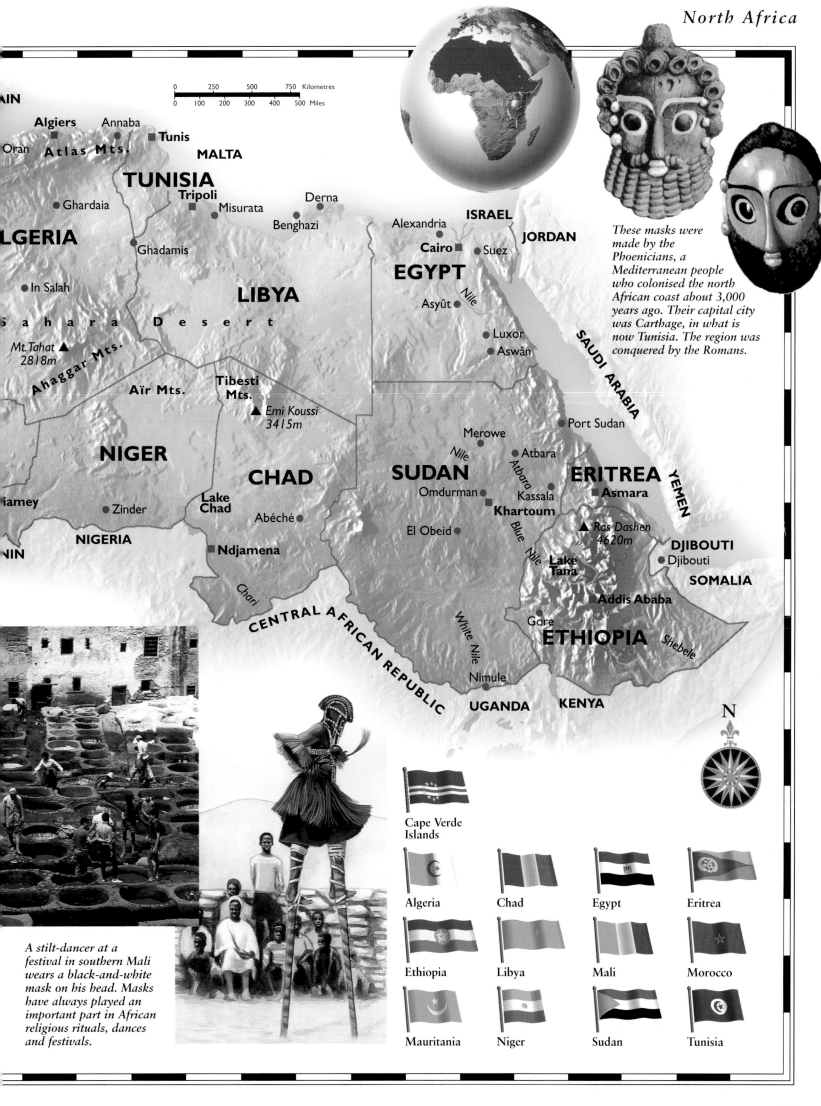

These masks were made by the Phoenicians, a Mediterranean people who colonised the north African coast about 3,000 years ago. Their capital city was Carthage, in what is now Tunisia. The region was conquered by the Romans.

A stilt-dancer at a festival in southern Mali wears a black-and-white mask on his head. Masks have always played an important part in African religious rituals, dances and festivals.

Cape Verde Islands

Algeria

Chad

Egypt

Eritrea

Ethiopia

Libya

Mali

Morocco

Mauritania

Niger

Sudan

Tunisia

63

West Africa

The lands around the Atlantic coast and the Gulf of Guinea are hot and very humid. They are crossed by great rivers such as the Sénégal, Gambia, Volta and Niger. Behind the sand bars and surf of the coast are forests, swamps and fertile plantation land which produces cocoa, rubber, cotton, peanuts and palm oil. Farther inland are plateaus and grazing lands, but in the far north the pasture is thin, and dust blows south from the Sahara desert. The region includes priceless mineral resources, such as oil in Nigeria, gold in Ghana and diamonds in Sierra Leone.

Powerful empires and kingdoms grew up long ago in this part of Africa, but the arrival of Europeans in the 1500s led to a cruel trade in slaves to the Americas and a long period of rule by Great Britain and France. Independence from these colonial powers came in the 1950s, but economic and political problems followed, with periods of military rule. The largest and most powerful country in the region is Nigeria.

Okra stew is a popular dish in West Africa. When okra is stewed it becomes smooth and sticky. It may be served with prawns, saltfish, hotly spiced meat or yam chips.

The dense forests and lagoons of the Niger delta region, here at Wari, are rich in oil and are a major source of wealth for the Nigerian government. Local people have protested about the pollution of their environment by the oil companies and their lack of a share in the profits.

Togo is home to various peoples, including the Ewe, Kabre and Mina. Many keep up their cultural traditions. These dancers from Togo wear beaded kilts, horns, necklaces and armlets. Dance and music play an important part in life throughout Africa, and African drumming has influenced the popular music of the Americas.

Cotton is an important crop in West African countries such as Guinea-Bissau, Togo, Benin, Nigeria and Burkina Faso.

Northern West Africa is mostly Muslim, while the south is mostly Christian. This Catholic cathedral was built at Yamoussoukro, Côte d'Ivoire, in 1989. It is called Our Lady of Peace. It cost millions of dollars in a country where many people are desperately poor.

This ritual dance is being performed by Cameroon's 'voodoo queens'. They follow African religions which believe in a world of spirits. Voodoo beliefs travelled from West Africa to the Americas in the days of the slave trade. Today about a quarter of all Cameroonians follow spirit beliefs.

Peoples and languages

West Africa is home to very many different ethnic groups, such as the Wolof, Mende, Kru, Mossi, Ewe, Hausa, Fulani, Ibo and Yoruba. Liberia and Sierra Leone were settled in the 1800s by Africans freed from the slave trade across the Atlantic.

Many different languages are heard in West Africa, and many people can speak either English or French, the languages of the colonial period, in addition to their own tongue. Colonial languages are still used in many schools, law courts and businesses.

Portuguese is spoken in Cape Verde and Guinea-Bissau, and Spanish in the small country of Equatorial Guinea.

A colourful textile from Benin features local animal life – a bull, a chameleon, a snake and two fruit bats.

0 100 200 300 400 500 600 700 Kilometres
0 100 200 300 400 Miles

MAURITANIA

SENEGAL
■ Dakar

GAMBIA
Banjul ■

Bissau

GUINEA-
BISSAU

MALI

GUINEA

Conakry ■

Freetown ■

SIERRA LEONE

Monrovia ■

LIBERIA

BURKINA
FASO

Ouagadougou ■

CÔTE
D'IVOIRE

GHANA

Yamoussoukro ■

Abidjan ●

Accra ■

Benue

BENIN

TOGO

Lomé ■

Lagos ●

Porto Novo ■

NIGER

Kano ●
Kaduna ●

Ibadan ●

NIGERIA

Niger

■ Abuja

Port Harcourt ●

BIOKO

Douala ●
■ Yaoundé

CAMEROON

CHAD

CENTRAL
AFRICAN
REPUBLIC

EQUATORIAL GUINEA ■ Mbini

SÃO TOMÉ
AND PRÍNCIPE

Libreville ●

GABON

CONGO

DEMOCRATIC REPUBLIC OF CONGO

Brazzaville ■

ANGOLA

N

The president's palace in Dakar, the capital of Senegal. After the country became independent from France in 1960, it remained under the rule of President Léopold Senghor for 20 years. Today it is a democracy. The Senegalese economy depends on peanuts, fish-processing and chemicals.

Crops such as maize or millet are pounded into flour with heavy pestles. Many African peoples make porridges, mashes or drinks from these grains. West African women often lead very busy lives, cooking, working in the fields and selling produce such as yams, peanuts or palm oil at market.

Côte d'Ivoire

Benin

Cameroon

Congo

Gabon

Gambia

Ghana

Guinea

Liberia

Nigeria

Senegal

Sierra Leone

Togo

Burkina Faso

Guinea Bissau

Equatorial Guinea

São Tomé and Príncipe

Central and East Africa

The river Congo drains a vast area of rainforest on its journey to the Atlantic coast. The river and the network of waterways that flow into it provide useful transport routes for riverboats and canoes. The country of the Democratic Republic of Congo lies on the Equator and has a hot and humid climate, with torrential rains and thunderstorms. It has a fertile soil and rich deposits of copper, cobalt, zinc, manganese and diamonds. Three-quarters of the land is covered by forest. In recent years the country suffered a severe civil war, but this ended in 1997 when rebel forces took control.

To the north, in the Central African Republic, the rainforest gives way to grasslands and dry plateaus. To the east are volcanic mountain ranges and the two small nations of Rwanda and Burundi, both of which have also suffered tragic civil wars.

A great crack in the Earth's crust, the Great Rift Valley, runs through East Africa. Its course is marked by mountains, gorges and deep lakes. Uganda, Kenya and Tanzania take in fertile highlands, savannah (grassy plains dotted with trees) and desert regions. The Indian Ocean coast is lined with white beaches, palm trees and coral islands. East Africa produces sugar-cane, mangoes, coffee and sisal.

Some people in Central and East Africa lead very traditional lives, such as the Masai who herd cattle on the grasslands of Kenya and Tanzania. Others live and work in busy, modern cities, such as Nairobi.

A garden amongst the rooftops on the island of Zanzibar, just north of Dar-es-Salaam. Zanzibar has been part of Tanzania since 1974, and is famous for spices, especially cloves, and for its large wooden sailing vessels called dhows.

Two women from the Democratic Republic of Congo exchange gossip as they braid their hair in elaborate styles. Central and East African fashions feature colourful, boldly patterned cotton wraps tied around the waist.

Kilimanjaro towers above the savannah of the Kenya-Tanzania border. At 5,950 metres above sea level, it is the highest mountain in Africa, but even in this region of burning heat, its summits are covered in snow.

The Makonde people live on the coast and southern borders of Tanzania. They are skilled wood carvers. Hundreds of different ethnic groups live in Central and East Africa, each with their own customs and language. East Africa has also been settled, during its history, by Arabs, Indians and European colonialists.

Lions often hunt by night, and spend the day sleeping in the shade and playing with their cubs. These big cats hunt the great herds of zebra and wildebeeste which still roam the African savannah. Many are protected within wildlife reserves.

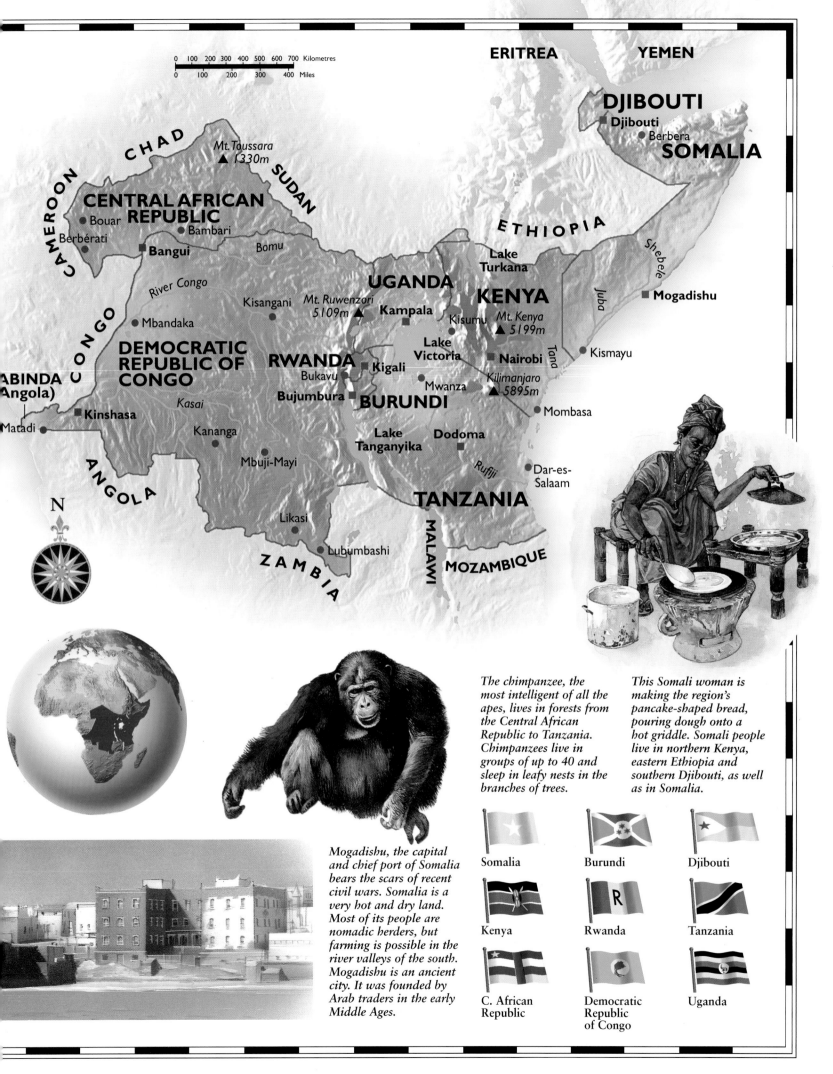

0 100 200 300 400 500 600 700 Kilometres
0 100 200 300 400 Miles

ERITREA   YEMEN

DJIBOUTI
Djibouti
Berbera
SOMALIA

CHAD

Mt. Toussara
▲ 1330m

CENTRAL AFRICAN
REPUBLIC

CAMEROON

Bouar
Berbérati   Bambari

Bangui   Bomu

SUDAN

River Congo

Kisangani   Mt. Ruwenzori   Kampala
5109m ▲

Mbandaka

ETHIOPIA

Shebele

Lake
Turkana

UGANDA   KENYA

Kisumu   Mt. Kenya
▲ 5199m

Juba

Mogadishu

CONGO

DEMOCRATIC
REPUBLIC OF
CONGO

RWANDA

ABINDA
(Angola)

Kasai

Kinshasa

Matadi

Bukavu   Kigali

Bujumbura   BURUNDI

Lake
Victoria   Nairobi

Kismayu

Tana

Mwanza   Kilimanjaro
▲ 5895m

Mombasa

Kananga

Lake
Tanganyika   Dodoma

Mbuji-Mayi

Rufiji

Dar-es-
Salaam

ANGOLA

TANZANIA

Likasi

Lubumbashi

ZAMBIA

MALAWI

MOZAMBIQUE

N

The chimpanzee, the most intelligent of all the apes, lives in forests from the Central African Republic to Tanzania. Chimpanzees live in groups of up to 40 and sleep in leafy nests in the branches of trees.

This Somali woman is making the region's pancake-shaped bread, pouring dough onto a hot griddle. Somali people live in northern Kenya, eastern Ethiopia and southern Djibouti, as well as in Somalia.

Mogadishu, the capital and chief port of Somalia bears the scars of recent civil wars. Somalia is a very hot and dry land. Most of its people are nomadic herders, but farming is possible in the river valleys of the south. Mogadishu is an ancient city. It was founded by Arab traders in the early Middle Ages.

Somalia   Burundi   Djibouti

Kenya   Rwanda   Tanzania

C. African
Republic   Democratic
Republic
of Congo   Uganda

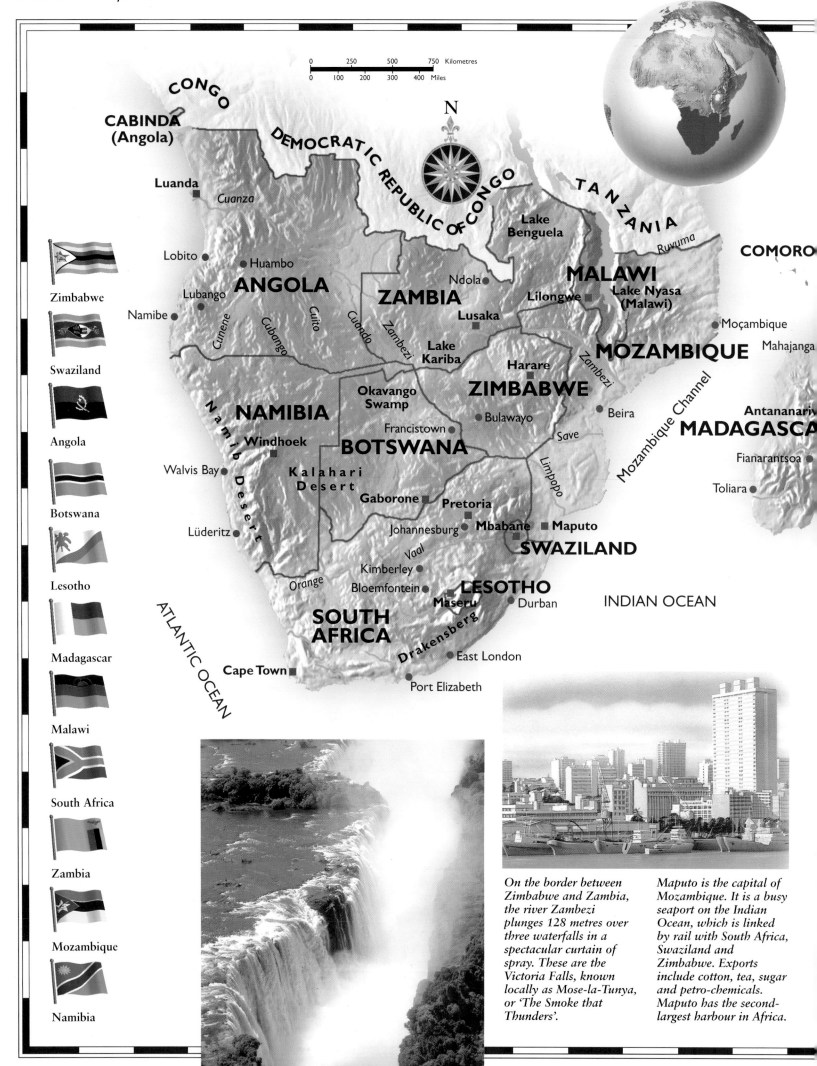

CABINDA
(Angola)

CONGO

DEMOCRATIC REPUBLIC OF CONGO

TANZANIA

N

COMORO

Luanda
Cuanza

Lake
Benguela

Ruvuma

Lobito
Huambo

MALAWI

ANGOLA

ZAMBIA

Ndola

Lilongwe
Lake Nyasa
(Malawi)

Lubango

Namibe

Lusaka

Moçambique

Mahajanga

Cunene

Cubango

Cuito

Cuando

Zambezi

Lake
Kariba

MOZAMBIQUE

Harare

Zambezi

Okavango
Swamp

ZIMBABWE

NAMIBIA

Bulawayo

Beira

Mozambique Channel

MADAGASCA

Antananari

Namib Desert

Windhoek

Francistown

BOTSWANA

Save

Fianarantsoa

Walvis Bay

K a l a h a r i
D e s e r t

Limpopo

Toliara

Gaborone

Pretoria

Lüderitz

Johannesburg
Mbabane

Maputo

SWAZILAND

Vaal

Kimberley

LESOTHO

INDIAN OCEAN

ATLANTIC OCEAN

Orange

Bloemfontein

Maseru

Durban

SOUTH
AFRICA

Drakensberg

East London

Cape Town

Port Elizabeth

Zimbabwe

Swaziland

Angola

Botswana

Lesotho

Madagascar

Malawi

South Africa

Zambia

Mozambique

Namibia

On the border between Zimbabwe and Zambia, the river Zambezi plunges 128 metres over three waterfalls in a spectacular curtain of spray. These are the Victoria Falls, known locally as Mose-la-Tunya, or 'The Smoke that Thunders'.

Maputo is the capital of Mozambique. It is a busy seaport on the Indian Ocean, which is linked by rail with South Africa, Swaziland and Zimbabwe. Exports include cotton, tea, sugar and petro-chemicals. Maputo has the second-largest harbour in Africa.

Southern Africa

Diamonds are mined in South Africa and Namibia. The region has very rich mineral resources, including copper in Zambia, gold in South Africa and uranium in Namibia. The world's largest diamond was found in South Africa in 1905.

Antseranana

bamasina

Southern Africa includes grasslands known as veld, great swamps such as the Okavango and harsh deserts such as the Namib and Kalahari. The region has high mountains and beautiful lakes and its beaches border the southern waters of the Atlantic and Indian oceans. Africa's biggest island, Madagascar, lies across the Mozambique Channel. Southern Africa has a rich wildlife including antelope, lions and elephants. Madagascar is famous for its lemurs.

Southern Africa produces many crops, including grapevines, citrus fruits, wheat, maize and tobacco. Cattle ranching is important for the economy of Botswana.

Peoples of the region include the Herero, Tswana, Khoi-San, Ndebele, Shona, Zulu, Xhosa, Swazi and Sotho. Minorities are descended from Dutch, English and Asian settlers. The most powerful and wealthy country of the region is South Africa. For many years this country was ruled by white-only governments. Black and Asian citizens were not allowed to vote. Today South Africa has become a democracy, and its first black president, Nelson Mandela, was elected in 1994.

A Comoros woman wears a white make-up made of wood ground against coral and mixed to a pulp. It protects and cleanses the skin. Comoros islanders are descended from Africans, Arabs and Southeast Asian peoples. The islands produce spices and exquisite perfume oils.

This girl is carrying a load of maize husks. Many Zambian women work long hours on small farms and garden plots where they grow maize, sorghum, millet and a starchy root called cassava to feed their families. Other crops are grown on a larger scale for export. They include sugar-cane, cotton and tobacco.

Fruits of Zimbabwe include mangoes, passion fruit, juicy pineapples and delicious avocado pears. They grow well in the country's hot, tropical climate, which is milder on the high plateaus and hills.

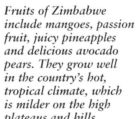

The forests of Madagascar were once home to a wide variety of wildlife. However much of the island has now been stripped bare by farmers and logging companies. Without roots to hold it in place, the soil is soon washed away by tropical rains. The government has started to plant new forests to stop this happening.

South Africa's 19th-century parliament buildings are in the southern city of Cape Town. Since 1994 they have housed a multi-racial democratic government. The largest political parties include the African National Congress, the National Party and Inkatha Freedom Party.

There are 90 species of chameleon and most of these live in tropical Africa, including Madagascar. Chameleons are large lizards with swivelling eyes and long sticky tongues. They are able to change their colour for camouflage. Their long tails and toes wrap around twigs and branches.

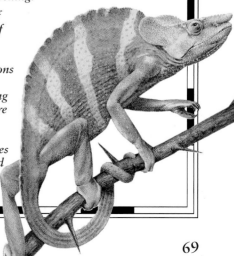

Australia

Australia

Australia is an island so huge that it is normally considered to be a continent in its own right. It stretches from the sub-tropical forests of the north to the cool seas of Tasmania, far to the south. Australia is bordered in the northeast by 2,027 kilometres of coral, the Great Barrier Reef. This is the haunt of sharks and beautiful tropical fish. While the 'outback', the remote lands of the interior, is famed in Australian history, most Australians today are town-dwellers.

Eastern and southern coasts are the site of large cities such as Brisbane, Sydney, Melbourne and Adelaide. Many rivers rise in the Great Dividing Range, which runs parallel to the coast. Inland are grasslands, largely given over to sheep stations and cattle ranches. These give way to eucalyptus forest, dry scrub, burning deserts and rocks. Beyond the vast Nullarbor Plain is Perth, the largest city in Western Australia.

Australia became an island so long ago that many of its animals, such as kangaroos and koalas, are seen nowhere else on Earth. Aboriginals, expert hunters and travellers, have lived in Australia for at least 40,000 years.

The dense rainforest of the Lamington Plateau, to the south of Brisbane, is a haven for rare animals and plants. It was made a National Park in 1915 and today is popular with bush-walkers, campers and nature-lovers.

Darwin Arnhem Land

Gulf Carpent

Kimberley Plateau

Broome

Fitzroy

Great Sandy Desert

NORTHERN TERRITORY

Barkl Tablela

AUSTRALIA

Alice Springs

Ashburton

Carnarvon

Gibson Desert

▲ Uluru (Ayers Rock) 867m

Alberga

Sim Des

WESTERN AUSTRALIA

Murchison

Great Victoria Desert

SOUTHERN AUSTRALIA

L E

Geraldton

Nullarbor Plain

Lak Torre

Kalgoorlie

★Perth
Fremantle

N

Great Australian Bight

Adelaide

| 0 | 100 | 200 | 300 | 400 | 500 | 600 | Kilometres |
| 0 | | 100 | | 200 | | 300 | Miles |

Surf's up! The rolling waves of the Pacific Ocean are perfect for surfing. Australia's sunny climate makes it ideal for sport and outdoor pursuits.

Boomerangs were first used for hunting by Australia's Aboriginals. When thrown in the air, the boomerang curves back towards the thrower. Aboriginal crafts and bark paintings are highly valued as works of art.

A Pacific power

In 1788 the British founded a prison colony in New South Wales. Settlers then seized the land from the Aboriginals, many of whom were attacked and killed. Many more European immigrants arrived over the years. Only in recent years have Aboriginals gained full rights as citizens.

Australia built its wealth on vast mineral reserves and on exports of wool and meat. Today it is one of the leading economic powers of the Pacific. Australia is still ruled by the British monarch, but there are growing calls for the country to become a republic.

Cape York Peninsula

Mitchell

Cairns

Great Barrier Reef

Norman

Townsville

Flinders

Great Dividing Range

QUEENSLAND

nantina

SOUTH PACIFIC OCEAN

Warrego

● Rockhampton

Brisbane ★

Darling

NEW SOUTH WALES

Great Dividing Range

Lachlan

● Newcastle

Murray

★ Sydney

CANBERRA (A.C.T.)

VICTORIA ▲ Mt Kosciusko 2228m

★ Melbourne

Bass Strait

TASMANIA

★ Hobart

Sydney Harbour is known for two famous landmarks – its opera house and its bridge. The skyscrapers belong to the city's business district, which borders the green spaces of the Royal Botanic Garden.

Canberra is Australia's purpose-built capital. Its new parliament buildings, on Capital Hill, were opened in 1988. Australia is governed on a federal basis, with some of its laws being passed nationally, and others regionally by its eight states and territories.

Australian Aboriginals play the didgeridoo, a long, hollow wooden instrument which makes a deep, droning, whirring sound.

Lamingtons are sponge squares coated in chocolate and coconut – a tasty snack at tea-time. Australia's many different immigrants have brought their own styles of cooking with them, whether Greek, Italian or Thai.

New Zealand

The beautiful islands of New Zealand lie in the southwest Pacific Ocean, about 2,000 kilometres from Australia. They have a mild, often cool, climate.

North Island is the most populated part of the country. Here are the two large cities of Auckland and Wellington. This is a land of fertile plains, rising to a central plateau and eastern mountains. The island has three active volcanoes as well as bubbling hot springs and spectacular geysers (gushers of water heated by volcanic rocks, deep under the ground).

Across Cook Strait is South Island, with its high ridge of mountains, the Southern Alps. Aorangi-Mount Cook is 3,764 metres above sea level. Over the ages glaciers have scraped out deep sea inlets in the southwest. To the east are the fertile Canterbury Plains and the hills of Otago. The chief southern cities are Christchurch and Dunedin. Further south lies mountainous Stewart Island, across the Foveaux Strait, and to the east are the Chatham Islands.

New Zealand's unspoiled coasts and mountains are ideal for outdoor pursuits such as sailing and climbing. New Zealanders are keen sports enthusiasts and are world leaders at rugby football.

Tuataras are large, lizard-like creatures, the only surviving members of their reptile family. They were once common in New Zealand but now are found only on a few islands off the coast. They live in burrows and hunt insects by night. Unlike most reptiles, tuataras can remain active in temperatures as low as 7°C.

North Cape

N

Whangarei

Auckland

Hamilton

Waikato

Rotorua

Lake Taupo

Gisborne

New Plymouth

Mt. Egmont
2518m

Mt. Ruapehu
▲ 2797m

NORTH ISLAND

Napier

Hastings

NEW ZEALAND

Wanganui

Palmerston North

Nelson

■ WELLINGTON

Blenheim

SOUTH PACIFIC OCEAN

Greymouth

Tasman Sea

Southern Alps

Aorangi-Mount Cook ▲
3764m

Rakaia

Christchurch

SOUTH ISLAND

Timaru

Waitaki

Milford Sound

Lake Te Anau

Clutha

Dunedin

New Zealand

Invercargill

STEWART ISLAND

| 0 | 50 | 100 | 150 | 200 | Kilometres |

| 0 | 50 | | 100 | Miles |

Peoples of the islands

The first New Zealanders were the Maoris, a Polynesian people who settled the islands from about AD800 onwards. They hunted moas, the large flightless birds which then lived there, collected shellfish, grew sweet potatoes and built forts called *pa*. New Zealand became a British colony in 1840.

The Maoris were soon cheated of their lands by the European settlers who rushed to New Zealand when gold was discovered in 1861. New Zealand became independent in 1907, but retained strong links with Britain. In the past 20 years it has seen itself more as one of the Pacific trading nations.

Most New Zealanders are English-speakers of European descent. Maoris make up about 10 percent of the population, and there are other Polynesian settlers such as Cook Islanders. Farming is the mainstay of the economy. Major exports include wool and lamb, butter and cheese, apples and pears.

A geyser bursts into the air at Whaka-rewarewa, near Rotorua on North Island. The energy from New Zealand's hot rocks is harnessed to generate electric power. Geysers and hot springs also attract tourists who are fascinated by the forces of nature.

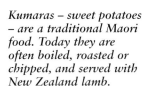

Kumaras – sweet potatoes – are a traditional Maori food. Today they are often boiled, roasted or chipped, and served with New Zealand lamb.

The flightless kiwi is an emblem of New Zealand. With its long bill, it hunts for insects amongst fallen leaves in the forest. New Zealand has no native mammals, and so its birds never needed to fly away from attack.

Wellington is the New Zealand capital. It is a seaport, built on the southwestern tip of North Island. It is also a centre for business and communications, and manufactures machinery, chemicals, soap and vehicles.

New Zealand has many fast-flowing rivers and large lakes, filled by melting snows. They are used to generate electricity. Three-quarters of all power comes from the country's 30 hydroelectric schemes. Lake Roxburgh in the Otago region of South Island, has been dammed so that its waters can drive powerful turbines. New Zealand also uses coal, oil, natural gas, geothermal energy and natural steam in its power stations.

Farming is an essential part of the New Zealand economy. For every person who lives there, there are thought to be 20 animals. Sheep, like those shown here on a farm in Cambridge, North Island, are the most important livestock. New Zealand lamb and wool are famous throughout the world.

Giant wetas are huge, flightless crickets. There are various species. They have been hunted by rats and other rodents brought to New Zealand by human beings, and are now only found on some offshore islands.

Pacific Islands

Pago Pago is a port of call for Pacific shipping and the heart of the fishing industry. Sited on Tutuila island, it is the capital of American Samoa. Here, fishing crews are unloading a catch of tuna, bound for the island's seafood canneries.

The Pacific Ocean is the largest expanse of water in the world, covering an area of about 180,000,000 square kilometres. It has deep sea trenches, volcanic islands and coral reefs.

The settlement of the scattered island chains of the Pacific was an amazing feat of sailing and exploration, which took place between 4,000 and 1,000 years ago. Inhabitants of the region today include Melanesians, Micronesians, Polynesians and groups of European or Asian descent. Many islanders have kept up ancient customs and traditions, such as dancing, singing, the weaving of garlands and public feasting.

Many of the Pacific islands came under foreign rule in the 1700s and 1800s. Since the 1960s some of these have formed new, independent nations such as Kiribati, Tuvalu and Vanuatu. Many Pacific islanders live by fishing, growing tropical fruits, coconuts and root crops such as taro. Most of the islands are very beautiful and some attract tourists. Others, however, have been stripped by phosphate mining or blasted by the testing of nuclear weapons.

Papua New Guinea, which shares its island home with Irian Jaya, the easternmost province of Indonesia, has valuable copper reserves on Bougainville, and its warm, humid climate is ideal for growing timber, cocoa and coffee. The French territory of New Caledonia also has rich mineral reserves, but most Pacific islands have little land or resources.

This dish, known as unu bona boroma, *is eaten in Papua New Guinea. It is made from boiled slices of breadfruit served with bacon, onions and chicken stock.*

The world's largest butterfly is the rare Queen Alexandra's birdwing of Papua New Guinea. It lives in rainforests in the north. The wingspan of females may be a staggering 28 cm or more.

East China Sea

WAKE ISLAND (U.S.A.)

NORTHERN MARIANA ISLANDS (U.S.A.)

Philippine Sea

GUAM (U.S.A.)

PALAU   **FEDERATED STATES OF MICRONESIA**

NAURU

IRIAN JAYA (INDONESIA)   **PAPUA NEW GUINEA**   **SOLOMON ISLANDS**

Arafura Sea

Port Moresby

VANUATU

Coral Sea

NEW CALEDONIA (Fr.)

AUSTRALIA

N

Tasman Sea

NEW ZEALAND

Micronesia

Marshall Islands

Fiji

Kiribati

Tuvalu

Nauru

Vanuatu

Papua New Guinea

Samoa

Palau

Solomon Islands

Tonga

NORTH
AMERICA

MIDWAY ISLAND
(U.S.A.)

NORTH PACIFIC
OCEAN

MEXICO

HAWAII
(U.S.A.)

MARSHALL
ISLANDS

KIRIBATI

GALÁPAGOS
(Ecuador)

SOUTH
AMERICA

ALU

SAMOA

AMERICAN
SAMOA
(U.S.A.)

COOK
ISLANDS
(N.Z.)

FRENCH POLYNESIA
(Fr.)

FIJI

TONGA

PITCAIRN ISLAND
(U.K.)

EASTER ISLAND
(CHILE)

SOUTH PACIFIC
OCEAN

| 0 | 500 | 1000 | 1500 | 2000 Kilometres |
| 0 | 250 | 500 | 750 | 1000 | 1250 Miles |

Huge statues (right) called moai *were raised on Easter Island about 1,000 years ago. The island was the home of Polynesian people, who believed that the statues had mysterious powers. Today, Easter Island is governed by Chile, 4,000 kilometres to the east.*

A villager from the Goroka region of Papua New Guinea wears a mud mask in the image of an evil spirit. The masks were once worn to scare enemies, but today are worn only at feasts.

A craftsman (left) carves a tiki, *a stone figure from one of the myths of the ancient Polynesians. He comes from the island of Nuku Hiva, one of the Marquesas chain in French Polynesia. Traditional crafts include carving in stone, wood and whalebone.*

A woman from Kiribati, in the central Pacific, puts together strips of matting made from fronds of the coconut palm. Coconuts provide food, fibre and roofing materials. They are dried to make copra, one of the Pacific region's most important exports.

The Polar Lands

The northernmost and southernmost points on Earth are called the Poles. Around them are bitterly cold, permanently frozen lands, swept by icy winds. While it is winter at the North Pole, it is summer at the South Pole. Polar summers are short, with no proper darkness, while the winters are long, with little daylight. The skies sometimes flicker with glowing lights called 'aurorae'.

Antarctica is the fifth largest continent. It is a land of mountains and glaciers, white with dazzling snow and ice. Even the sea is frozen solid. In places the Antarctic ice sheet is nearly 5 kilometres thick. Great flat-topped icebergs break off from the ice shelf and drift through the Southern Ocean. Antarctica is the windiest place on Earth and has some of the lowest temperatures on record. Birds nest on the icy coasts and fish and whales swim offshore, but no mammals live on the frozen lands around the South Pole.

No people live here permanently. There are bases visited by teams of scientists. Several countries claim territories in Antarctica and the land is rich in minerals. However, more and more people are calling for Antarctica to be left unspoiled, the last true wilderness on Earth.

Melting ice floats off the shores of Antarctica. Some scientists believe that the Earth's climate is becoming warmer. If the polar ice sheets melted, sea levels would rise around the world and cause flooding.

The Emperor penguin is one of six penguin species which breed in Antarctica. Its sleek coat protects it against the bitterly cold waters where it catches fish.

The first person to reach the South Pole was the Norwegian explorer Roald Amundsen, on 14 December 1911. He used dogs to pull sleds of supplies across the ice.

SOUTH ATLANTIC OCEAN

INDIAN OCEAN

Antarctic Peninsula

Queen Maud Land

Enderby Land

Weddell Sea

Ronne Ice Shelf

Trans-Antarctic Mountains

▲ *Vinson Massif* 5140m

● **South Pole**

Ellsworth Land

0 200 400 600 800 1000 1200 1400 Kilometres
0   200   400   600   800 Miles

Ross Ice Shelf

▲ *Mt. Erebus* 3,800m

Victoria Land

Wilkes Land

Ross Sea

SOUTH PACIFIC OCEAN

Antarctic Circle

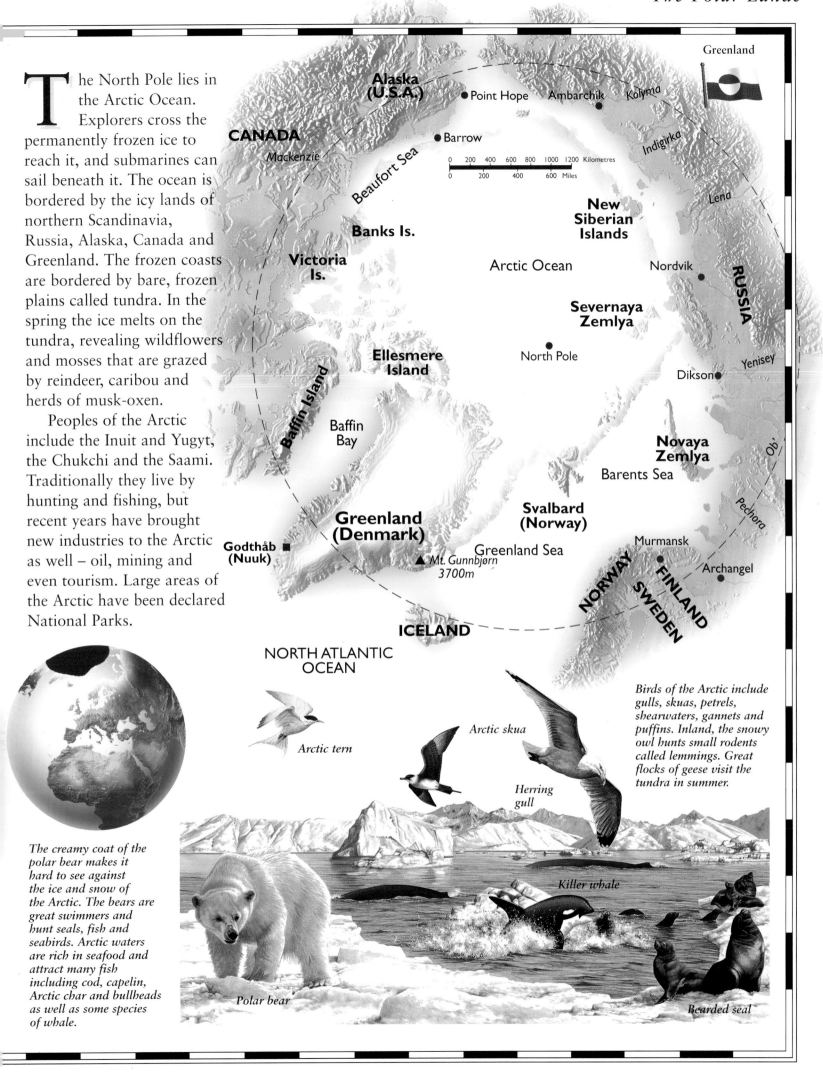

The North Pole lies in the Arctic Ocean. Explorers cross the permanently frozen ice to reach it, and submarines can sail beneath it. The ocean is bordered by the icy lands of northern Scandinavia, Russia, Alaska, Canada and Greenland. The frozen coasts are bordered by bare, frozen plains called tundra. In the spring the ice melts on the tundra, revealing wildflowers and mosses that are grazed by reindeer, caribou and herds of musk-oxen.

Peoples of the Arctic include the Inuit and Yugyt, the Chukchi and the Saami. Traditionally they live by hunting and fishing, but recent years have brought new industries to the Arctic as well – oil, mining and even tourism. Large areas of the Arctic have been declared National Parks.

Greenland

Alaska (U.S.A.)
● Point Hope
Ambarchik
Kolyma
CANADA
Mackenzie
● Barrow
Indigirka
Beaufort Sea
Lena
New Siberian Islands
RUSSIA
Banks Is.
Arctic Ocean
Nordvik
Victoria Is.
Severnaya Zemlya
North Pole
Yenisey
Ellesmere Island
Dikson ●
Baffin Island
Novaya Zemlya
Baffin Bay
Barents Sea
Ob
Svalbard (Norway)
Pechora
Murmansk
Greenland (Denmark)
Greenland Sea
Archangel
Godthåb (Nuuk) ■
▲ Mt. Gunnbjørn 3700m
NORWAY
FINLAND
SWEDEN
ICELAND

0 200 400 600 800 1000 1200 Kilometres
0 200 400 600 Miles

NORTH ATLANTIC OCEAN

Arctic tern

Arctic skua

Herring gull

Birds of the Arctic include gulls, skuas, petrels, shearwaters, gannets and puffins. Inland, the snowy owl hunts small rodents called lemmings. Great flocks of geese visit the tundra in summer.

Killer whale

The creamy coat of the polar bear makes it hard to see against the ice and snow of the Arctic. The bears are great swimmers and hunt seals, fish and seabirds. Arctic waters are rich in seafood and attract many fish including cod, capelin, Arctic char and bullheads as well as some species of whale.

Polar bear

Bearded seal

North America

Facts and Figures

Country	Area (sq km)	Population	Capital	Official language	Currency	Major products
Antigua and Barbuda	442	62,000	St. John's	English	East Caribbean dollar	Oil products
Bahamas	13,935	262,000	Nassau	English	Bahamian dollar	Oil products
Barbados	431	259,000	Bridgetown	English	East Caribbean dollar	Sugar, oil products, electrical goods, clothing
Belize	22,965	198,000	Belmopan	English, Spanish	Belize dollar	Sugar, bananas, citrus products, fish, clothing
Canada	9,976,130	27,445,000	Ottawa	English, French	Canadian dollar	Wheat, natural gas, oil, wood pulp, newsprint, iron ore, cars and parts, fish
Costa Rica	50,700	3,099,000	San José	Spanish	Colon	Coffee, bananas, manufactured goods
Cuba	114,524	10,822,000	Havana	Spanish	Peso	Sugar, tobacco
Dominica	751	72,000	Roseau	English	East Caribbean dollar	Citrus fruits, bananas
Dominican Republic	48,734	7,471,000	Santo Domingo	Spanish	Peso	Sugar, coffee
El Salvador	21,041	5,396,000	San Salvador	Spanish	Colon	Coffee, cotton
Grenada	344	91,000	St. George's	English	East Caribbean dollar	Cocoa, nutmeg, mace, bananas
Guatemala	108,889	9,745,000	Guatemala City	Spanish	Quetzal	Coffee, bananas, cotton, beef
Haiti	27,750	6,764,000	Port-au-Prince	French	Gourde	Coffee, bauxite, sugar
Honduras	112,088	5,462,000	Tegucigalpa	Spanish	Lempira	Coffee, bananas, timber, meat
Jamaica	10,991	2,469,000	Kingston	English	Jamaican dollar	Bauxite, alumina
Mexico	1,972,547	89,538,000	Mexico City	Spanish	Peso	Oil, coffee, cotton, sugar, manufactured goods
Nicaragua	130,000	4,130,000	Managua	Spanish	Cordoba	Cotton, coffee, meat, chemicals
Panama	75,650	2,515,000	Panama	Spanish	Balboa	Bananas, shrimps, sugar, oil products
St. Christopher (St. Kitts) and Nevis	262	42,000	Basseterre	English	East Caribbean dollar	Sugar
St. Lucia	616	137,000	Castries	English	East Caribbean dollar	Bananas, cocoa, citrus fruits, coconuts, tourism

Country	Area (sq km)	Population	Capital	Official language	Currency	Major products
St. Vincent and the Grenadines	388	109,000	Kingstown	English	East Caribbean dollar	Bananas, arrowroot, coconuts
Trinidad and Tobago	5,130	1,265,000	Port-of-Spain	English	Trinidad dollar	Oil, asphalt, chemicals, sugar, fruit, cocoa, coffee
United States of America	9,363,123	255,020,000	Washington D.C.	English	US dollar	Machinery, vehicles, aircraft and parts, iron and steel goods, coal, chemicals, cereals, soya beans, textiles, cotton

South America

Facts and Figures

Country	Area (sq km)	Population	Capital	Official language	Currency	Major products
Argentina	2,766,889	33,101,000	Buenos Aires	Spanish	Peso	Meat and meat products, tobacco, textiles, leather, machinery
Bolivia	1,093,581	7,832,000	La Paz (Seat of government); Sucre (Legal capital)	Spanish	Boliviano	Tin, oil, natural gas, cotton
Brazil	8,511,965	156,275,000	Brasilia	Portuguese	Real	Machinery, vehicles, soya beans, coffee, cocoa
Chile	765,945	13,599,000	Santiago	Spanish	Peso	Wood pulp, paper, copper, timber, iron ore, nitrates
Colombia	1,138,914	33,424,000	Bogota	Spanish	Peso	Coffee, emeralds, sugar, oil, meat, skins and hides
Ecuador	283,561	10,741,000	Quito	Spanish	Sucre	Oil, bananas, cocoa, coffee
French Guiana	91,000	104,000	Cayenne	French	French franc	Bauxite, shrimps, bananas
Guyana	214,000	808,000	Georgetown	English	Guyanese dollar	Sugar, rice, bauxite, alumina, timber
Paraguay	406,752	4,519,000	Asuncion	Spanish	Guarani	Cotton, soya beans, tobacco, timber
Peru	1,285,216	22,454,000	Lima	Spanish	Sol	Metals, minerals (silver, lead, zinc, copper), fish
Suriname	163,265	438,000	Paramaribo	Dutch, English	Guilder	Bauxite, alumina, rice, citrus fruit
Uruguay	176,216	3,131,000	Montevideo	Spanish	Peso	Meat, wool, hides and skins
Venezuela	912,050	20,249,000	Caracas	Spanish	Bolivar	Oil, iron, cocoa, coffee

Europe

Facts and Figures

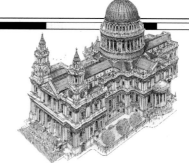

Country	Area (sq km)	Population	Capital	Official language	Currency	Major products
Albania	28,748	3,363,000	Tirana	Albanian	Lek	Oil, bitumen, metals, tobacco, fruit and vegetables
Andorra	453	47,000	Andorra la Vella	Catalan	French franc	Tourism, postage stamps
Austria	83,849	7,884,000	Vienna	German	Schilling	Food, iron and steel, textiles, paper products, machinery
Belarus	207,600	10,321,000	Minsk	Belorussian, Russian	Rouble	Lorries and tractors, fertilizers, flax, computers
Belgium	30,513	9,998,000	Brussels	Flemish, French	Belgian franc	Chemicals, vehicles, machinery, iron, steel
Bosnia-Herzegovina	51,129	4,397,000	Sarajevo	Serbo-Croat	Dinar	Timber, textiles, corn, wheat, barley, bauxite, iron ore, coal
Bulgaria	110,912	8,963,000	Sofia	Bulgarian	Lev	Metals, machinery, textiles, tobacco, food
Croatia	56,537	4,808,000	Zagreb	Serbo-Croat	Kuna	Chemicals, textiles, aluminium products, paper, wine, bauxite
Czech Republic	77,864	10,404,000	Prague	Czech	Koruna	Machinery, timber, wheat, beer, animals, coal, uranium
Denmark	45,069	5,170,000	Copenhagen	Danish	Krone	Food, machinery, metals and metal goods
Estonia	45,100	1,542,000	Tallinn	Estonian	Kroon	Textiles, shipbuilding, mining equipment, dairy products
Finland	337,009	5,042,000	Helsinki	Finnish, Swedish	Markka	Wood and wood pulp, paper, paperboard, machinery
France	547,026	57,372,000	Paris	French	French franc	Cars, electrical equipment, wine, cereals, textiles, leather goods, chemicals, iron, steel
Germany	356,755	80,569,000	Berlin	German	Deutsch-mark	Manufactured goods, chemicals, consumer goods, engineering goods
Greece	131,944	10,300,000	Athens	Greek	Drachma	Manufactured goods, food, wine, tobacco, chemicals
Hungary	93,030	10,313,000	Budapest	Hungarian	Forint	Transport equipment, electrical goods, bauxite
Iceland	103,000	260,000	Reykjavik	Icelandic	Krona	Fish products
Ireland, Republic of	70,283	3,547,000	Dublin	English, Irish	Irish pound (punt)	Meat and meat products, dairy products, beer, whiskey
Italy	301,252	57,782,000	Rome	Italian	Lira	Machinery, motor vehicles, iron and steel, textiles, shoes
Latvia	65,200	2,632,000	Riga	Latvian	Lats	Electric railway cars, telephone exchanges, dairy produce

Country	Area (sq km)	Population	Capital	Official language	Currency	Major products
Liechtenstein	157	28,000	Vaduz	German	Swiss franc	Cotton yarn and material, screws, bolts, needles
Lithuania	65,200	3,759,000	Vilnius	Lithuanian	Litas	Cattle, electric motors and appliances, cereals
Luxembourg	2,586	390,000	Luxembourg City	French, Letzebuergesh	Luxembourg franc	Iron and steel, chemicals, vehicles, machinery
Macedonia	25,713	2,050,000	Skopje	Macedonian	Denar	Chemicals, machinery, food
Malta	316	359,000	Valletta	Maltese, English	Maltese pound	Food, manufactured goods, ship repairing, tourism
Moldova	33,700	4,394,000	Chisinau	Romanian	Leu	Machinery, food processing, vines, fruit and vegetables
Monaco	1.9	28,000	Monte Carlo	French	French franc	Tourism
Netherlands	40,844	15,178,000	Amsterdam	Dutch	Guilder	Oil, chemicals, food and animals, machinery
Norway	324,219	4,286,000	Oslo	Norwegian	Krone	Animal products, paper, fish, metals, metal products, oil
Poland	312,677	38,365,000	Warsaw	Polish	Zloty	Lignite, coal, coke, iron and steel, ships, textiles, food
Portugal (inc. Azores and Madeira)	92,082	9,846,000	Lisbon	Portuguese	Escudo	Textiles, timber, cork, wine, machinery, chemicals, sardines
Romania	237,500	23,185,000	Bucharest	Romanian	Leu	Food, machinery, minerals, metals, oil, gas, chemicals
Russia	17,075,400	149,469,000	Moscow	Russian	Rouble	Wheat, timber, oil, textiles, minerals, metals, coal, gas
San Marino	61	23,000	San Marino	Italian	Italian lira	Wine, cereals, cattle, tourism, postage stamps
Slovakia	49,035	5,287,000	Bratislava	Slovak	Koruna	Manufactured goods, corn, wheat, timber, iron ore
Slovenia	20,251	1,985,000	Ljubljana	Slovenian	Tolar	Textiles, steel, wheat, potatoes, mercury, coal
Spain	504,782	38,085,000	Madrid	Spanish	Peseta	Manufactured goods, chemicals, textiles, leather, fish, wine, fruit
Sweden	449,964	8,678,000	Stockholm	Swedish	Swedish krona	Timber, machinery, metals, metal products, cars
Switzerland	41,288	6,905,000	Bern	French, German, Italian, Romansh	Swiss franc	Tourism, machinery, chemicals and pharmaceuticals, watches, food, textiles
Ukraine	603,700	52,200,000	Kiev	Ukranian	Hryvna	Iron and steel, machinery, vehicles, sugar, coal, iron ore
United Kingdom	244,828	57,848,000	London	English	Pound sterling	Manufactured goods, electrical engineering, textiles, chemicals
Vatican City State	0.44	1000	Vatican City	Italian, Latin	Italian lira	
Yugoslavia (Serbia & Montenegro)	102,173	19,394,000	Belgrade	Serbo-Croat	Dinar	Chemicals, clothing, food, iron and steel, machinery

Asia

Facts and Figures

Country	Area (sq km)	Population	Capital	Official language	Currency	Major products
Afghanistan	647,497	19,062,000	Kabul	Pashtu, Dari (Persian)	Afghani	Skins, cotton, natural gas, fruit
Armenia	29,800	3,677,000	Yerevan	Armenian	Dram	Fruit and vegetables, tobacco, electrical engineering, tools
Azerbaijan	86,800	7,237,000	Baku	Azerbaijani	Manat	Cotton, grain, oil, chemicals, oil machinery
Bahrain	622	533,000	Manama	Arabic	Dinar	Oil
Bangladesh	143,998	119,288,000	Dhaka	Bengali	Taka	Jute, leather, hide and skins, tea
Bhutan	47,000	1,612,000	Thimphu	Dzongkha, Nepali, English	Ngultrum	Rice, fruit, timber
Brunei	5,765	270,000	Bandar Seri Begawan	Malay	Brunei dollar	Oil
Cambodia	181,035	9,054,000	Phnom Penh	Khmer	Riel	Rice, rubber
China	9,596,961	1,187,997,000	Beijing (Peking)	Chinese (Mandarin)	Yuan	Industrial and agricultural products
Cyprus	9,251	716,000	Nicosia	Greek, Turkish	Pound	Fruit, vegetables, wine, manufactured goods, minerals
Georgia	69,700	5,482,000	Tbilisi	Georgian	Lary	Metallurgy, machinery, citrus fruit, electrical engineering, tea
India	3,287,590	879,000,000	New Delhi	Hindi, English	Rupee	Tea, industrial goods, jute, textiles
Indonesia	2,027,087	191,170,000	Jakarta	Bahasa (Indonesian)	Rupiah	Oil, palm products, rubber, coffee
Iran	1,648,000	56,964,000	Tehran	Persian (Farsi)	Rial	Oil, natural gas, cotton
Iraq	434,924	19,290,000	Baghdad	Arabic	Iraqi dinar	Oil, dates, wool, cotton
Israel	20,770	4,946,000	Jerusalem	Hebrew, Arabic	Shekel	Cut diamonds, chemicals, fruit, tobacco
Japan	372,313	124,336,000	Tokyo	Japanese	Yen	Optical equipment, ships, vehicles, machinery, electronic goods, chemicals, textiles
Jordan	97,740	4,291,000	Amman	Arabic	Jordanian dinar	Phosphates, fruit, vegetables
Kazakhstan	2,717,000	17,038,000	Aqmola	Kazakh	Tenge	Wheat, cotton, oil, gas, coal
Korea, North	120,538	22,618,000	Pyongyang	Korean	Won	Iron and other metal ores
Korea, South	98,484	43,663,000	Seoul	Korean	Won	Textiles, manufactured goods, chemicals

Country	Area (sq km)	Population	Capital	Official language	Currency	Major products
Kuwait	17,818	1,970,000	Kuwait City	Arabic	Kuwait dinar	Oil, Chemicals
Kyrgyzstan	198,500	4,533,000	Bishkek	Kyrgyz	Som	Sheep, wool, horses, yaks, silk, electrical engineering, carpet
Laos	236,800	4,469,000	Vientiane	Lao	Kip	Timber, coffee
Lebanon	10,400	2,838,000	Beirut	Arabic	Lebanese pound	Precious metals, gemstones
Macao	16	374,000	Macao	Portuguese, Chinese	Pataca	Light manufactured goods
Malaysia	329,749	18,181,000	Kuala Lumpur	Malay	Malaysian dollar	Rubber, tin, palm oil, timber
Maldive Islands	298	231,000	Male	Divehi	Rupee	Fish, copra
Mongolia	1,565,000	2,310,000	Ulan Bator	Mongolian	Tugrik	Cattle, horses, wool, hair
Myanmar (Burma)	676,552	43,668,000	Yangon (Rangoon)	Burmese	Burmese kyat	Teak, oil cake, rubber, jute
Nepal	140,797	20,577,000	Katmandu	Nepali	Rupee	Grains, hides, cattle, timber
Oman	212,457	1,637,000	Muscat	Arabic	Omani riyal	Oil, dates, limes, tobacco, frankincense
Pakistan	803,943	115,520,000	Islamabad	Urdu, English	Rupee	Cotton, carpets, leather, rice
Philippines	300,000	64,259,000	Manila	Filipino	Peso	Sugar, timber, coconut products
Qatar	11,000	453,000	Doha	Arabic	Qatar riyal	Oil
Saudi Arabia	2,149,690	15,922,000	Riyadh	Arabic	Riyal	Oil
Singapore	581	2,812,000	Singapore	Malay, Chinese, Tamil, English	Singapore dollar	Refined oil products, electronic goods, rubber
Sri Lanka	65,610	17,405,000	Colombo	Sinhala	Rupee	Tea, rubber, coconut products, industrial goods
Syria	184,480	12,958,000	Damascus	Arabic	Syrian pound	Cotton, oil, cereals, animals
Taiwan	35,961	20,300,000	Taipei	Chinese (Mandarin)	Taiwan dollar	Textiles, electrical goods, plastics, machinery, food
Tajikistan	143,100	5,568,000	Dushanbe	Tajik	Rouble	cotton, vines, silk, carpets, aluminium
Thailand	514,000	57,760,000	Bangkok	Thai	Baht	Rice, tapioca, rubber, tin
Turkey	780,576	58,775,000	Ankara	Turkish	Turkish lira	Cotton, tobacco, nuts, fruit
Turkmenistan	488,100	3,859,000	Ashgabat	Turkmen	Manat	Cattle, sheep, lambskins, carpets, oil refining, gas
United Arab Emirates	83,600	1,629,000	Abu Dhabi	Arabic	Dirham	Oil, natural gas
Uzbekistan	447,400	21,363,000	Tashkent	Uzbek	Som	Chemicals, gas, cotton

Country	Area (sq km)	Population	Capital	Official language	Currency	Major products
Vietnam	329,556	69,306,000	Hanoi	Vietnamese	Dong	Fish, coal, agricultural goods
Yemen	527,968	9,400,000	San'a	Arabic	Dinar	Cotton, coffee, hides and skins, fish, refined oil

Africa

Facts and Figures

Country	Area (sq km)	Population	Capital	Official language	Currency	Major products
Algeria	2,381,741	26,346,000	Algiers	Arabic	Algerian dinar	Natural gas, oil
Angola	1,246,700	10,609,000	Luanda	Portuguese	Kwanza	Coffee, diamonds, oil
Benin	112,522	4,918,000	Porto Novo	French	Franc CFA	Cocoa, cotton
Botswana	600,372	1,373,000	Gaborone	English, Setswana	Pula	Copper, diamonds, meat
Burkina Faso	274,200	9,490,000	Ouagadougou	French	Franc CFA	Livestock, groundnuts, cotton
Burundi	27,834	5,786,000	Bujumbura	French, Kirundi	Burundi franc	Coffee
Cameroon	475,442	12,198,000	Yaounde	English, French	Franc CFA	Cocoa, coffee, oil
Cape Verde Islands	4,033	384,000	Praia	Portuguese	Escudo	Bananas, fish
C. African Republic	622,984	3,173,000	Bangui	French	Franc CFA	Coffee, diamonds, timber
Chad	1,284,000	5,961,000	N'Djamena	French	Franc CFA	Cotton, cattle, meat
Comoros	2,171	585,000	Moroni	French	Franc CFA	Spices
Congo	342,000	2,368,000	Brazzaville	French	Franc CFA	Oil, timber
Côte d'Ivoire	322,463	12,910,000	Yamoussoukro	French	Franc CFA	Cocoa, coffee, timber
Democratic Republic of Congo	2,345,409	39,882,000	Kinshasa	French	Congo franc	Coffee, cobalt, copper
Djibouti	22,000	467,000	Djibouti	French	Djibouti franc	Cattle, hides and skins
Egypt	1,001,449	55,163,000	Cairo	Arabic	Egyptian pound	Cotton, oil, textiles
Equatorial Guinea	28,055	369,000	Malabo	Spanish	Franc CFA	Cocoa, coffee, timber
Eritrea	117,600	3,318,000	Asmera	No official language	Ethiopian birr in use	Hides, salt, cement
Ethiopia	1,104,300	50,527,000	Addis Ababa	Amharic	Birr	Coffee, hides and skins
Gabon	267,667	1,237,000	Libreville	French	Franc CFA	Manganese, oil
Gambia	11,295	878,000	Banjul	English	Dalasi	Groundnuts
Ghana	238,537	15,959,000	Accra	English	Cedi	Cocoa, gold, timber

Country	Area (sq km)	Population	Capital	Official language	Currency	Major products
Guinea	245,957	6,116,000	Conakry	French	Guinean franc	Alumina, bauxite
Guinea-Bissau	36,125	1,006,000	Bissau	Portuguese	Guinea-Bissau peso	Fish, groundnuts
Kenya	582,646	26,985,000	Nairobi	English, Swahili	Kenya shilling	Coffee, tea, hides
Lesotho	30,355	1,836,000	Maseru	English, Sesotho	Loti	Wool, mohair
Liberia	111,369	2,580,000	Monrovia	English	Liberian dollar	Iron ore, rubber
Libya	1,759,540	4,875,000	Tripoli	Arabic	Libyan dinar	Oil
Madagascar	587,041	12,827,000	Antananarive	French, Malagasy	Malgache franc	Coffee, spices, vanilla
Malawi	118,484	8,823,000	Lilongwe	English, Chichewa	Kwacha	Tobacco, tea
Mali	1,240,000	9,818,000	Bamako	French	Mali franc	Groundnuts, cotton
Mauritania	1,030,700	2,143,000	Nouakchott	Arabic, French	Ouguiya	Iron ore, copper
Mauritius	2,085	1,084,000	Port Louis	English	Rupee	Sugar, tea, tobacco
Morocco	446,550	26,318,000	Rabat	Arabic	Dirham	Phosphates, fruit
Mozambique	783,030	14,872,000	Maputo	Portuguese	Metical	Sugar, fruit, vegetables
Namibia	824,292	1,534,000	Windhoek	English	Rand	Minerals, diamonds, fish
Niger	1,267,000	8,252,000	Niamey	French	Franc CFA	Groundnuts, livestock, uranium
Nigeria	923,768	115,664,000	Abuja	English	Naira	Oil, palm kernels, cocoa
Rwanda	26,338	7,526,000	Kigali	French, Kinyar–wanda	Rwanda franc	Coffee
São Tomé and Príncipe	965	124,000	São Tomé	Portuguese	Dobra	Cocoa
Senegal	196,192	7,736,000	Dakar	French	Franc CFA	Groundnuts, phosphates
Seychelles	280	72,000	Victoria	English, French	Rupee	Copra, fish, spices
Sierra Leone	71,740	4,376,000	Freetown	English	Leone	Diamonds, iron ore
Somalia	637,657	9,204,000	Mogadishu	Somali	Somali shilling	Livestock
South Africa	1,221,037	42,327,000	Pretoria (Government); Cape Town (legal capital)	Afrikaans, English and nine African languages	Rand	Gold, diamonds, fruit, vegetables
Sudan	2,505,813	26,656,000	Khartoum	Arabic	Sudanese dinar	Cotton, groundnuts
Swaziland	17,363	792,000	Mbabane	English	Lilangeni	Sugar, wood pulp, asbestos, fruit
Tanzania	945,087	27,829,000	Dodoma	English, Swahili	Tanzanian shilling	Coffee, cotton, sisal, spices

Country	Area (sq km)	Population	Capital	Official language	Currency	Major products
Togo	56,000	3,763,000	Lome	French	Franc CFA	Phosphates, cocoa, coffee
Tunisia	163,610	8,401,000	Tunis	Arabic	Tunisian dinar	Phosphates, olive oil, oil
Uganda	236,036	18,674,000	Kampala	English	Uganda shilling	Coffee, cotton
Zambia	752,614	8,638,000	Lusaka	English	Kwacha	Copper
Zimbabwe	390,580	10,583,000	Harare	English	Zimbabwe dollar	Tobacco

Australasia

Facts and Figures

Country	Area (sq km)	Population	Capital	Official language	Currency	Major products
Australia	7,686,849	17,529,000	Canberra	English	Australian dollar	Cereals, meat, sugar, honey, fruit, metals and mineral ores, wool
Fiji	18,274	739,000	Suva	English, Fijian	Fiji dollar	Sugar, coconut oil
Kiribati	931	74,000	Tarawa	English, Gilbertese	Australian dollar	Copra, phosphates, fish
Marshall Islands	181	50,000	Majuro	Marshallese, English	US dollar	Copra, sugar, coffee
Micronesia	701	114,000	Palikir	English	US dollar	Fruit (including coconuts), vegetables
New Zealand	268,676	3,414,000	Wellington	English	New Zealand dollar	Meat, dairy products, wool, fruit
Papua New Guinea	461,691	4,056,000	Port Moresby	English	Kina	Copra, cocoa, coffee, copper
Samoa	2,842	158,000	Apia	English, Samoan	Tala	Copra, cocoa, bananas
Solomon Islands	28,446	342,000	Honiara	English	Solomon Islands dollar	Timber, fish, copra, palm oil
Tonga	699	97,000	Nuku'alofa	English	Paíanga	Copra, bananas
Tuvalu	25	12,000	Fongafala	English, Tuvalu	Australian dollar	Copra
Vanuatu	14,763	157,000	Port Vila	Bislama, English, French	Vatu	Copra, fish

Index

Page numbers in
italic refer to the
illustrations

Acknowledgements

The publishers wish to thank the artists who have contributed to this book. These include the following:

Hamesh Alles; Julie Banyard; Harry Clow; Sandra Doyle; Chris Forsey; Mark Franklin; Jared Gilbey; Jeremy Gower/B.L.Kearley; Ray Grinaway; Mark Iley; Mike Lacey; Peter Massey; Steve Noon; Nicki Palin; Liz Sawyer/Simon Girling Associates; Clive Spong/Linden Artists; John Storey

The publishers wish to thank the following for supplying photographs for this book: Page 14, 15 Canadian High Commission; 16 ZEFA; 19 ZEFA; 20 (CL) ZEFA; 20 (C) Robert Harding Picture Library; 21 (TL) ZEFA; 21 (CL) Comstock Photo Library; 21 (BR) ZEFA; 22 (TR) Panos Pictures; 22 (CR) Robert Harding Picture Library; 24 (CL) Comstock Photo Library; 24 (CR) Robert Harding Picture Library; 25 (TL) Spectrum Colour Library; 26 (CL) Robert Harding Picture Library; 27 ZEFA; 28 (TL) Spectrum Colour Library; 28 (BL) ZEFA; 29 (TL) Comstock Photo Library; 30 (TR) Walter Mayr/Focus/Colorific!; 30 (CL) Gerald Buthaud/ Cosmos/Colorific!; 31 (BR) Dr Eckart Pott/Bruce Coleman Ltd.; 32 (CL) Spectrum Colour Library; 32 (CR) Spectrum Colour Library; 32 (BL) ZEFA; 34 (TR) Penny Tweedie/Colorific! 34 (CL) Steve Benson/ Colorific!; 34 (C) Stewart Galloway/Comstock Photo Library; 34 (BL) ZEFA; 36 (TL) Comstock Photo Library; 36 (CR) ZEFA; 36 (C) Disneyland Paris; 36 (BR) ZEFA; 38 (TR) Thomas Buchholz/Bruce Coleman Ltd; 40 (BR) Robert Harding Picture Library; 40 (BL) Comstock Photo Library; 42 (CL) Robert Harding Picture Library; 42 (B) ZEFA; 43 (BR) Robert Harding Picture Library; 44 (CL) J.Allan Cash; 44 (C) ZEFA; 44 (CR) ZEFA; 46 (CL) Spectrum Colour Library; 46 (BL) Spectrum Colour Library; 46 (CR) Robert Harding Picture Library; 46 (BR) Robert Harding Picture Library; 48 (CL) Spectrum Colour Library; 48 (TR) Peter Turnley/Black Star/Colorific!; 50 (BC) Heather Crossley; 52 (BL) World Pictures/Feature-Pix Colour Library; 52 (BR) Michael Short/Robert Harding Picture Library; 53 (TR) Robert Harding Picture Library; 54 (C) ZEFA; 54 (CL) ZEFA; 54 (CB) Spectrum Colour Library; 57 (BL) ZEFA; 57 (CR) Spectrum Colour Library; 57 (BR) Heather Crossley; 58/9 (TR) Japanese National Tourist Office; 59 (TR) ZEFA; 59 (C) Japanese National Tourist Office; 59 (BC) Spectrum Colour Library; 59 (BR) Spectrum Colour Library; 60 (TL) K.Helbig/ZEFA; 60 (BR) Spectrum Colour Library; 60 (C) Spectrum Colour Library; 62 (BL) Jeremy A Horner/ The Hutchison Library; 62 (BR) ZEFA; 64 (TR) Robert Harding Picture Library; 64 (C) Crispin Hughes/The Hutchison Library; 65 (BL) Sarah Errington/The Hutchison Library; 66 (CR) The Hutchison Library; 66 (TL) Tim Beddow/The Hutchison Library; 68 (CB) Comstock Photo Library; 69 (CR) Tim Beddow/The Hutchison Library; 71 ZEFA; 73 (C) The Hutchison Library; 75 (BL) New Zealand Tourist Board; 75 (TR) R.Ian Lloyd/Robert Harding Picture Library; 76 (TR) Spectrum Colour Library.